Fr. Marwos B

D1250391

The
Splendor
of
Pentecost

Dom E. Flicoteaux, O.S.B.

The
Splendor
of
Pentecost

Translated from the French by

MARY LOUISE HELMER

HELICON PRESS · *Baltimore, 1961*

Originally published in French by Les Editions du Cerf, under the title "Le Rayonnement de la Pentecôte."

Library of Congress Catalog Card Number 61-11759

Nihil Obstat: EDWARD A. CERNY, S.S., S.T.D.
Censor Librorum

Imprimatur: ✠ FRANCIS P. KEOUGH, D.D.
Archbishop of Baltimore
March 6, 1961

The *Nihil Obstat* and *Imprimatur* are official declarations that a book or pamphlet is free of doctrinal or moral error. No implication is contained therein that those who have granted the *Nihil Obstat* and *Imprimatur* agree with the opinions expressed.

PRINTED IN THE UNITED STATES OF AMERICA BY THE NORTH
CENTRAL PUBLISHING COMPANY, ST. PAUL, MINNESOTA

Preface

THE RECENT MEASURES TAKEN BY THE SACRED
Congregation of Rites concerning the Easter vigil cause us to hope
that the Feast of Easter will gradually regain the incontestable pre-
eminence that rightfully belongs to it in Christian devotion. Furthermore, similar measures taken for the celebration of Thursday
and Friday of Holy Week equally serve to emphasize the profound
significance, up to now too much forgotten, of this Feast of Feasts.
To be complete and definitive, however, the desired restoration of
the paschal solemnity requires that the Christian community have
a better understanding of the relation between Pentecost and
Easter. For, in the eyes of the Church, Pentecost is not only a
favorable time, fifty days after Easter, for honoring the third
Person of the Holy Trinity. It is above all the indispensable and
glorious crowning of Easter — the high point, so to speak, of the
work of the Redemption and the beginning of its universal
radiance.

Originally, as we have said elsewhere, the fifty paschal days
commemorated all together, *per modum unius,* the successive
stages of the unique mystery of the Redemption: the death and
Resurrection of Christ, His glorious Ascension and the pouring
out of His Spirit. Later, it is true, each of these events was separately celebrated on the anniversary of its historical occurrence.
This is why the descent of the Holy Ghost upon the Apostles is
commemorated on the fiftieth day after Easter. But, even though
they are celebrated separately, the Feast days of Easter and Pentecost continue to join each other liturgically in the unity of the
same mystery, the paschal mystery. The Church Fathers strongly

insisted on the link which unites the Feast of Easter to that of Pentecost. According to Saint Augustine, it is on the day of Pentecost that the solemnity of Easter comes to its end without losing any of its brilliance, and if Easter is the beginning of Grace, Pentecost is its crown. "Today," declares Saint John Chrysostom in a homily on Pentecost, "we have come to the summit of all good, we have arrived at the center of all solemnities." The ancient liturgies likewise stress the relationship between Pentecost and the feast of Easter, of which it is but the fullness. It is certain that the liturgical excitement of the Easter season, far from flagging, as one so often imagines that it does as the passing days leave Easter behind, on the contrary does nothing but grow and become more pronounced up to the end of the fifty-days period.

We trust that this book devoted to the subject of Pentecost will prove a useful supplement to the volume which we published in this series under the title "The Triumph of Easter" (*Le Triomphe de Pâques*). Above all, we wish to revive interest in a feast whose importance is impossible to exaggerate since it brings to a close the paschal solemnity only to assure its liturgical effulgence. First we will show, in Part One, that during the fifty days the Church prepares us, by perceptible and constant stages, to celebrate the descent of the Paraclete as the necessary and glorious completion of the work of the Redemption.

We shall then see, in Part Two, how each year there is brought about anew in the entire Church, by the celebration of the Mystery of Pentecost, an unstinted pouring out of the Holy Ghost. And finally, in Part Three, we shall see how the Spirit of Pentecost never ceases to aid the Church in her pilgrimage here below nor to glorify Christ through the sanctification of His members.

Abbaye Sainte-Marie des Deux-Montagnes, Canada
DEDICATED TO THE ARCHANGEL, ST. MICHAEL

CONTENTS

PART ONE

Before Pentecost

I

Paschal Liturgy and
The Perspective of Pentecost

IN OUR BOOK ON THE TRIUMPH OF EASTER WE
have already indicated that the paschal liturgy follows a very perceptible and continuous line from the Sunday of the Resurrection
to Pentecost.[1] Whereas during the first two weeks after Easter the
Church mostly speaks of the Resurrection of the Saviour and
our participation in this mystery through Baptism, after the third
Sunday of the paschal time, *Jubilate* Sunday, she is mainly concerned with quickening the desire of all her members to follow
the risen Christ up to the glory of heaven. It is true that the Epistle
of the night of Easter already exhorts all the baptized, that is, all
those who have participated in the Resurrection of Our Saviour,
to "Seek the things that are above, where Christ is seated at the
right hand of God. Mind the things that are above, not the things
that are on earth." [2] However, it is only from the third Sunday on
that the Church dwells upon the return of Our Saviour to His
Father in order to remind us that we, in turn, must join in heaven
the One Who has opened the gateway to our real native country.
The return of the glorified Christ to His Father, this is the thought
that becomes predominant in this new phase of the paschal liturgy; and its expression is all the more emphasized as one approaches nearer to the Feast of the Ascension. If, during the
fortnight that follows Easter, the Church applies herself principally to strengthening our faith in Christ as victor over death, and
to making us aware of the riches of our Baptism, it is apparent that
during the weeks preceding the Ascension the Church strives even

3

more to maintain and develop in our souls the hope of joining our Head there where He sits now at the right hand of the Father: *ubi Christus est in dextera Dei sedens.*

It is an undeniable fact that from the third Sunday after Easter the different liturgical texts of the breviary and the missal invite us with an obvious insistence to turn from worldly things, the *terrena,* and to attach ourselves preferably to the things of heaven, the *coelestia,*[3] so that from here below our minds and hearts may be fixed where true joys dwell. Moreover, we can easily see that the Masses of the three Sundays before the Ascension show a striking similarity as regards prayers, readings and hymns.

However, it should be carefully noted that in this second phase of the paschal time which ends with the Ascension of the Saviour, the Church already prepares us to celebrate the feast of the fiftieth day, the Ascension being only — as we shall have occasion to say later — the prelude to Pentecost. Between these two historical events, the return of Christ to heaven and the pouring out of the Holy Ghost on earth, the link is so close that, in the thought of God, so to speak, they form but one and the same mystery. And we may rightly consider the paschal time, as it develops progressively from Easter Sunday up to the feast of Pentecost, as the liturgical preparation for this final solemnity, "which completes the paschal work because of the fullness of the mystery which it contains."[4]

2

The Imminent Departure of the
Saviour towards Heaven
and the Promise of His Return

ACCORDING TO A TRADITIONAL ARRANGEMENT the reading of the fourth Gospel, begun around the middle of Lent, then interrupted intentionally during the Holy Week and the Octave of Easter,[1] in order to be resumed on Whitsunday, is followed regularly until Pentecost.

The different passages of this Gospel which still appear today in our Roman missal have been obviously chosen in connection with the liturgical development of the fifty days of the paschal period. This is evident as regards the two first Sundays after Easter.[2] As for the selections read on each of the following three Sundays, it is not without reason that all three are taken, though with a curious transposition, from the same chapter of St. John, Chapter 16, where the only question discussed is the return of Christ to His Father, and the coming of the Paraclete which will be the consequence of His return.[3] In the mind of the Church these readings have the obvious purpose of preparing us for the liturgical feasts of Ascension and Pentecost and of revealing to us the singular importance of these two mysteries from the point of view of our own glorification. Undoubtedly, in the fourth Gospel, the conversation in Chapter 16 precedes the account of the Passion, but we know that the Passion was always presented by the Saviour Himself as the first stage of His triumphal return to His Father, the preliminary phase of His glorification.[4]

5

Vado ad Patrem, "I go to the Father," this is the affirmation of Christ with which the Gospel of the Third Sunday opens, an affirmation which the Church does well to give prominence to in many antiphons of the Mass and of the Office during this phase of the paschal time.[5]

In fact the Gospel account concerns the announcement made by the Saviour to His disciples of His imminent departure for Heaven:

"A little while and you shall see me no longer; and again a little while and you shall see me, because I go to the Father."

Some of the disciples therefore said to one another, "What is this He says to us, 'A little while and you shall not see me, and again a little while and you shall see me'; and 'I go to the Father'?"

They kept saying therefore, "What is this 'little while' of which He speaks? We do not know what He is saying."

But Jesus knew that they wanted to ask Him, and He said to them, "You inquire about this among yourselves because I said, 'A little while and you shall not see me, and again a little while and you shall see me.'

"Amen, amen, I say unto you, that you shall weep and lament, but the world shall rejoice; and you shall be sorrowful but your sorrow shall be turned into joy.

"A woman about to give birth has sorrow, because her hour has come. But when she has brought forth the child, she no longer remembers the anguish for her joy that a man is born into the world.

"And you therefore have sorrow now, but I shall see you again, and your heart shall rejoice, and your joy no one can take from you."

In the homily which is still read today in the night office of this same Sunday, St. Augustine comments as follows on this passage of the Gospel: "When He says, 'A little while and you shall see me no longer,' Christ speaks to those who see Him present in the flesh. He speaks to them that way because He must return to His Father, and because after the Ascension His disciples will no longer be able to see Him with their own eyes, such as they saw Him at the moment He was telling them these things. But when He adds, 'and again a little while and you shall see me,' it is to the

entire Church that He addresses Himself. . . . The Lord will not
tarry long in keeping His promise. Yes, again a little while and we
shall see Him there where we will have nothing more to ask, no
questions to pose, nothing hidden to learn any more." [6]

Thus in the thought of St. Augustine, and in this case in that of
the Church, these last words, "A little while and you shall see me
no longer," are an encouragement which the Saviour gives not
only to His Apostles, but also to all generations of Christians that
will follow one another up to the end of time.

Undoubtedly on the day of His Ascension Christ withdrew His
visible presence from the world, but in order to become manifest
again, and in all the brilliance of His divine glory, when the hour
of His last coming shall have arrived. St. Augustine observes that
this "little while" of which the Saviour speaks "seems a long time
to us because it still lasts, but when it will have passed, we will
grasp how short it was." [7]

The little time that will precede the return of the Saviour, His
glorious and definitive return, will seem all the longer to us because it also will be a time of tears for all those who, aspiring to
join Christ in His glory, will walk in His footsteps and share His
Passion. For the following warning of the Master is addressed to
us, no less than to the Apostles: "Amen, amen. I say unto you, that
you shall weep and lament, but the world shall rejoice."

However, in order to reassure us, the Saviour hastens to add,
"But your sorrow shall be turned into joy. A woman about to give
birth has sorrow, because her hour has come. But when she has
brought forth the child, she no longer remembers the anguish for
her joy that a man is born into the world. And you therefore have
sorrow now, but I shall see you again, and your heart shall rejoice,
and your joy no one can take from you." [8]

This warning of the Saviour concerns not only the Apostles, but
all Christians of the centuries to come. Thus it is fitting that the
Church, in the days preceding the Ascension, recall it to the minds
of all those who are committed to follow Christ. In fact the time
of trial was to begin for all His disciples as soon as the Saviour
reached heaven and sent the Paraclete down to earth. Until the
final coming the life of the Church here below will pass in sorrow
and tears, amidst a world which intoxicates itself with a joy as

deceptive as it is ephemeral. But Christ Himself has given us the certainty that these sufferings, like those of the woman in childbirth, are fruitful, for they will bring to the members of the Church a gladness which no one can take away from them. This will be the participation, pure and undarkened by shadow, in the beatitude of Christ glorified.

3

The Sending of the Paraclete
and its Consequences

Wᴴɪʟᴇ ᴛʜᴇ ᴍᴀsᴛᴇʀ sᴘᴏᴋᴇ ᴏғ ʀᴇᴛᴜʀɴɪɴɢ sᴏᴏɴ
to the One who had sent Him, and of the persecutions which
would befall them, the disciples remained gloomy and silent.[1] The
Saviour then immediately told them: "And now I am going to Him
who sent me, and no one of you asks me, 'Where art thou going?'
But because I have spoken to you of these things, sorrow has filled
your hearts."

The hour, then, had come for Christ to reveal to those around
Him the necessity for His departure: "But I speak the truth to
you; it is expedient for you that I depart. For if I do not go, the
Advocate (the Paraclete) will not come to you, but if I go, I will
send him to you."

We have already arrived at the fourth week after Easter, and
the paschal time moves toward its end. We can glimpse the two
great liturgical feasts of the Ascension and of Pentecost which we
prepare to celebrate successively on the fortieth and fiftieth day
after Easter. Now the Church is bent on pointing out that the
Saviour Himself has revealed to us the close link which unites these
two mysteries which can be said to be really one. In order to carry
out the plan established by Divine Wisdom it was necessary that
Christ first ascend in His heavenly glory and that at the same time
He withdraw His visible presence from His disciples so that the
Paraclete might be sent to the earth. Since the pouring out of the
Holy Spirit had to be the fruit of the Saviour's sacrifice and glorifi-
cation, it was important for this glorification to be accomplished.

9

It is only when seated at the right hand of His Father and invested with full power over heaven and earth that Christ, the Son of God become man, would assign to us the infinite merits of His Cross. Moreover, how could He make Himself spiritually present in the souls of His disciples in order to illuminate them, strengthen them and guide them if He did not, as a preliminary, remove Himself from the view of their eyes of flesh?

But the Saviour does not content Himself with revealing to those around Him that His departure is the indispensable condition for the coming of the promised and expected Paraclete.[2] He is bent on making more precise the role which the Holy Spirit will play here below, be it in regard to the world, or more directly in regard to His own disciples:

"And when he has come he will convict the world of sin, and of justice, and of judgment: of sin, because they do not believe in me; of justice, because I go to the Father, and you will see me no more; and of judgment, because the prince of this world has already been judged."

The Paraclete "will convict the world of sin" because He will make manifest the sin committed by the Jews in rejecting the Messias, a sin which all who refuse to recognize the Saviour and to align themselves under His law will continue to commit, up to the end of time. Then the Paraclete will convict the world of justice in the sense that He will testify in a striking manner, through the work of sanctification of which He will be the beginner here below, that Christ restored the reign of justice which had been destroyed by the sin of the first man. He will prove that Christ was not only the pre-eminent "Just,"[3] but that His mission was to re-establish justice on earth by reconciling us with God through His death and by becoming the source of justice and sanctity for all those who believe in Him.[4] The coming of the Paraclete will prove that the work of our justification through Christ has been completed, since the Saviour will have returned to His Father, and since it will no longer be possible for His Apostles to see Him with bodily eyes.[5] Finally, the Paraclete will bear witness against the world. From His coming to this earth below it will have to be concluded that the Prince of this world is already judged, or, otherwise expressed, that his reign is virtually condemned. It is evident that the restoration of justice can be accomplished on earth only through a final eviction of the one who, since the First Fall, has constituted an obstacle to the coming of the reign of God by jealously holding man under his baleful empire. Already, shortly before the Last Supper, knowing that His glorification was imminent, the Master has said to His disciples:

"Now is the judgment of the world; now will the prince of the world be cast out. And I, if I be lifted up from the earth, will draw all things to Myself." [6]

How can the Paraclete bear the triple witness of which the Saviour speaks? He will show it in the Church and through the Church where, up to the end of time, He will exercise His vivifying action. This will be, first of all, owing to the Apostles themselves. They, from the time that they will have received the Holy Ghost, on the day of Pentecost, will speak in His name and their message will resound to the very ends of the earth. By virtue of this same Spirit, they will accomplish marvelous things which will strikingly testify to Christ's victory, and do so to the confusion of His enemies. The successors of the Apostles will continue the work begun by the Twelve until the return of the saviour.

Here, now, is what the role of the Paraclete will be, according to the Master, as far as the disciples are directly concerned:

"Many things I have to say to you, but you cannot bear them now. But when he, the Spirit of Truth, has come, he will teach you all the truth. For he will not speak on his own authority, but whatever he will hear he will speak, and the things that are to come he will declare unto you. He will glorify me, because he will receive of what is mine and declare it to you."

Once He has descended upon the Apostles on the day of Pentecost, the Holy Ghost will become their inner Master, instructing them from within. In fact, it is at the moment when He must leave His disciples that the Saviour has many other things to tell them which they are not yet in a state to bear: *adhuc multa habeo vobis dicere, sed non potestis portare modo.* Despite the training which they have received from their Master, ever since they have lived close to Him, the Apostles remain quite carnal. Their minds are as

if covered by a veil and their own conception of Messianism remains wholly narrow and shortsighted.[7] The Paraclete's very mission will be to teach them the entire truth: *Cum autem venerit ille
Spiritus veritatis docebit vos omnem veritatem.*[8] From the moment
the Paraclete will have penetrated the minds of the disciples, He
will flood them with His light and clarify for them what they have
found obscure in Christ's teaching. He will make them understand
what, up till then, they have grasped only very superficially. He
will enlighten them about the meaning of the prophecies concerning Christ, about the place that is due to the Cross in the economy
of salvation, about the transcendence of the Messianic reign, and
about the full dimension of the work of Redemption.

Better still, the Holy Ghost will be given to the disciples to serve
as a guide, for He will introduce them to the full and whole truth,
not only by revealing the consequences of the Redemption to
them, even those which will be realized in a more or less distant
future (*quae ventura sunt*), but by communicating to them the
fruits of the Sacrifice of the Cross.[9] It is through the accomplishment of the divine promises and through the abundant pouring
out of the supernatural riches of which the Saviour has become,
in His own flesh, the inexhaustible source, that the Holy Ghost
will glorify Christ: *Ille me clarificabit quia de meo accipiet et
annuntiabit vobis.*[10]

The passage of the Gospel read at the Mass of the fifth Sunday
likewise sets in relief the consequences of Christ's glorification and
of the sending of the Paraclete:

At that time Jesus said to His disciples: "Amen, amen, I say to
you, if you ask the Father anything in my name, He will give it to
you. Hitherto you have not asked anything in my name. Ask, and
you shall receive, that your joy may be full. These things I have
spoken to you in parables. The hour is coming when I will no
longer speak to you in parables, but will speak to you plainly of
the Father."

In this passage, the Saviour suggests that on the day when, by
virtue of the Holy Ghost, He will have made Himself present in
the souls of His disciples, they will have a full knowledge of His
Father. Undoubtedly, during His public life, Christ never ceased

to speak to the Apostles about His Father, of His personal relation with Him. Nonetheless, He expressed Himself only by means of images and similes (*in proverbiis*), and always in a more or less veiled manner. So much so that the disciples had not yet been able to discover, in the person of their Master, the One who was the perfect image of the Father. "Have I been so long a time with you," said the Saviour to St. Philip, "and you have not known me?" [11] But the hour was coming when Christ, leaving all allegory aside, would reveal the Father by communicating His Spirit to the Apostles.[12]

In fact it is only after having received the Spirit of adoption that the disciples will be able to recognize the Father as Father and that they will even be able to invoke Him in the name of the Son. For only those who, possessing the Spirit of Christ, are incorporated in Christ can petition the Father in the name of the Son. When therefore the Paraclete will have descended upon them on the day of Pentecost, the disciples will be able to present themselves to the Father as His sons and address Him in all truth as "Our Father." Their prayer will be directly inspired by the Holy Ghost, or, rather, they will continue to express here below the prayer of Christ Himself. The Saviour will no longer need to substitute for them and to pray in their place. The prayer of the disciples like that of Christ will rise directly up to heaven. Jesus says so Himself:

"In that day you shall ask in My name; and I do not say to you that I will ask the Father for you, for the Father Himself loves you because you have loved Me, and have believed that I came forth from God.[13] I came forth from the Father and have come into the world. Again I shall leave the world and go to the Father."

What the Lord definitively wished to make known to His followers before leaving them was the profound change in our relations with God, now become our Father, which would result from the Ascension and the sending of the Paraclete. From now on, all that we ask of the Father in the name of the Son will be given to us: *si quid petieritis Patrem in nomine meo dabit vobis.* Then nothing more will be lacking in this filial joy of which the Holy Ghost will be the beginning: *et accipietis ut gaudium vestrum sit plenum.*

During the three weeks which precede the solemnity of the Ascension, the Church has given us a reading wholly, or nearly so, from the 16th Chapter of St. John. The Church thus reminds us of the place that is due to the Ascension of the Lord in the work of Redemption, progressively preparing us to celebrate its admirable mystery. From Christ's own lips we are able to learn of the close link which unites the Ascension to the Pentecost. He has clearly revealed to us that, of these two events, the first is the necessary condition for the second, and has made us aware of the sovereignly important consequences which derive therefrom, not only in an immediate way for the disciples, but for all future members of His Church.

4

Awaiting the Ascension

Everything was not over for Christ when, in the night of Easter, He was raised up as the victor over darkness and death. In order that His glorification be complete, it was still necessary that He ascend to heaven in order to sit there at the right hand of God. Likewise for us Christians, everything is not over on the day of Baptism when we are born to the life of the Christ raised up from the grave. For our redemption will not be accomplished before we have been able to join our Saviour in the glory of heaven corporally. If, therefore, on Easter day it be possible for us to celebrate our own resurrection by renewing ourselves in the purity of our baptism, we must still prepare ourselves — but this time by Hope — for the mystery of our future ascension towards the place where Christ Himself has already preceded us as our precursor.

Between His Resurrection and His return to the Father there elapsed a period of forty days, during which the Saviour appeared to His disciples and spoke to them about the kingdom of God.[1] Immediately after His baptism, as if in a prelude to His struggle against the powers of darkness which was to culminate in the victory of the Cross, Christ had already immersed Himself for forty days in the solitude of the desert. In imitation of their divine Model, Christians, each year, also prepare themselves, during the forty days of Lent, in penitence and prayer, for the celebration of the paschal triumph. If the risen Christ, before ascending to heaven, wished to remain on earth for forty days in order to be among His disciples, the reason must be sought in the biblical symbolism of this number forty, which is frequently employed in the Old Testament.[2] Undoubtedly the ideas with which it is asso-

15

ciated are not always the same. But, in general, the duration of
forty days or of forty years is that space of time which Scripture
attributes to an ordeal, a transitory state, or a short-lived enter-
prise, whether it be a punishment like the deluge,[3] or an arduous
trek like that of the Israelites towards the Promised Land.[4] The
preparation or the waiting for a decisive event likewise lasts forty
days. It is only at the end of forty days that David responded to
the provocations of Goliath.[5] Moses had to remain forty days and
forty nights on the top of Mt. Sinai before receiving the tables of
the covenant.[6]

Likewise the forty days that followed the Resurrection were,
for the Master and His disciples, a period of transition and waiting. While the Saviour readied Himself to return to His Father, He
completed the instruction of His disciples and prepared them for
the imminent coming of the Paraclete. Now, today, during this
same period of forty days, the Church prepares all Christians to
celebrate the mystery of Christ ascending to heaven. But she does
this by proposing this mystery to us as the beginning and the
pledge of our future ascension. Whereas the Gospels read at Mass
on the last Sundays after Easter shed a full light on the consequences of the Resurrection of the Saviour, His return to the
Father, and the sending of the Paraclete, the Epistles of these
same Sundays, taken either from St. Peter or from St. James, sug-
gest what the attitude of the baptized here below must be while
waiting for the day when they will be able to join Christ and
participate, in the very flesh, in His celestial glory.[7]

During these forty days that separate the feast of Easter from
that of the Ascension, all Christians are invited to fix their attention on heaven, their true native country. Therefore, according
to the recommendation made to us by St. Peter in the Epistle of
the third Sunday, we must conduct ourselves here below as
strangers and pilgrims (*tanquam advenae et peregrini*). Let us,
therefore, be prudent and guard ourselves against "carnal desires
which war against the soul." While they are sojourning in this
world the role of Christians is to bear to God, amidst a society
once more become pagan, the witness of an irreproachable conduct (*conversationem vestram inter gentes habentes bonam*) so
as to reduce to silence those senseless people who, out of foolish-

ness or malevolence, reject Christ and His law. Finally, for the real children of the celestial Father, it is a question of giving the world an example of a resolutely Christian life, rooted in a sincere and total submission to God and His legitimate representatives, even if they abuse their authority.[8] It is a question of Christians' showing respect for all persons (*omnes honorate*), of practicing brotherly love (*fraternitatem diligite*), of acting only in the filial fear of God (*Deum timete*). Such, according to St. Peter, is the program that all those who aspire to join Christ in the glory of heaven must follow.

The Collect of the third Sunday is visibly in harmony with the recommendations contained in the Epistle of this same day. For all those who, since their Baptism, publicly profess the Christian faith (*qui christiana professione consentur*), the Church petitions for grace to realize the life program traced by St. Peter, through an energetic rejection of everything that is incompatible with the title of Christian (*et illa respuere quae huic inimica sunt nomini*), and through the assiduous practice, on the contrary, of everything which honors it (*et ea quae sunt apta sectari*).

The readings of the two last Sundays after Easter are both taken from the Epistle of St. James, the second merely completing the teaching contained in the first. Now St. James expressly invites us to look above, where dwells the Father of Lights from Whom proceeds every perfect gift and every grace: *Omne datum optimum et omne donum perfectum desursum est descendens a Patre luminum*. It is, in fact, the Father of Lights Whom we prepare ourselves to receive on the day of Pentecost, a new pouring out of Him Who is the pre-eminent Gift, the substantial Gift of God most high: *Donum Dei altissimi*. The best means of preparing ourselves to receive the Holy Ghost is, as St. James exhorts, to accept the word of God with alacrity and docility, to guard ourselves against every defilement, every excess of malice, and to cherish in the depths of our being the doctrine that brings salvation to souls.

The Collect of the fourth Sunday also seems to echo the teaching of the Epistle. In fact, from this Father of Lights, in Whom there is no change nor shadow of alteration (*apud quem non est trans-*

mutatio, nec vicissitudinis obumbratio), the Church petitions that amid the continual agitations of this world (*inter mundanus varietates*) it become possible for us, in some measure, to share in the divine stability. To do this, must not our hearts remain fixed where real joys lie, that is to say, where we wish to join the glorified Christ?

However, it is not enough merely to accept the word of the Lord docilely. In his Epistle of the following Sunday, St. James tells us that Christ's word still — and above all — must be resolutely put into practice: *Estote factores verbi, et non auditores tantum.* For there can be no happiness here below except in the careful observation of the Gospel. But practicing the Gospel is, first, winning mastery over one's tongue. In fact the sins that are committed by the tongue are innumerable: lies and calumnies, idle talk, improper suggestions, insults and blasphemies. Nor can the Gospel be put into practice without the performance of good works. One must show oneself helpful towards the weak and towards all the disinherited of this world, such as orphans and widows in distress. Moreover, such good and merciful works are an excellent means of preserving perfect purity of heart against the world and its multiple temptations.

To be sure, the faithful observance of the commandments of the Lord would be impossible without the help of divine grace. Thus it is fitting that in the Collect of the fifth Sunday we petition God, not only to inspire us always with what is just, and conformable to His will (*ut cogitemus, te inspirante, quae recta sunt*), but to make us capable of carrying it out (*et, te gubernante, eadem faciamus*).

This is how the Church, by means of the paschal liturgy, and above all of the Eucharistic Sacrifice which is its very center, arranges all things so that we ourselves, by following Christ, may arrive at the glory of heaven to which He has opened the path for us: *Ut per haec pia devotionis officia ad coelestem gloriam transeamus.*[9]

5

The Glorious Ascension

UNFORTUNATELY TOO FEW CHRISTIANS ARE
aware of all that the Feast of the Ascension, so justly styled *glorious* [1] in the canon of the Mass and elsewhere, represents. For we
can be sure that it is not without cause that the Church has singled
out as "glorious" the Ascension of the Lord. At first sight, however, it seems that the word would be just as fitting, if not more so,
to describe the feast of Easter, "the solemnity of solemnities,"
since the Resurrection specifically marks the great triumph of the
Lord over hell and over death. On the other hand, the Passion,
which the canon of the Mass qualifies as "blessed," would also
have some title to be called "glorious." [2] Does not the Church herself sing that Christ has won His victory and merited His crown
through the wooden cross: *Regnavit a ligno Deus*? [3] Truth to tell,
is there any thing more triumphal than the liturgy of the feasts of
the Cross?

Then why does the Church reserve the qualification *glorious*
more especially for the Ascension of the Lord?

The scene of the Ascension, as it is presented to us by the Gospel,
transpired with an extreme simplicity. It was not, like the Trans-
figuration, accompanied by circumstances that bring that so mysterious episode in the life of Christ into such relief. On the day of
the Ascension, St. Luke tells us, Jesus "led them towards Bethany,
and He lifted up His hands and blessed them. And it came to pass
as He blessed them that He parted from them and was carried into
heaven." [4] In the no less brief description of the event preserved
in the book of the Acts, St. Luke simply notes that the Saviour,
after having been among His disciples, was lifted up and that a

cloud took him out of their sight. *Et cum hoc dixisset, videntibus illis, elevatus est, et nubes suscepit eum ab oculis eorum.*[5] Nothing more. No change was even pointed out in the very person of the Lord, who preserved, it seems, His habitual appearance for as long a time as His disciples could follow him with their sight. It was only when Christ had disappeared into the clouds of heaven that two angels, looking like men dressed in white garments, presented themselves to the amazed disciples in order to tell them that He would return in the same way as they had seen Him ascend.[6]

But with the Ascension it is as with the other great liturgical solemnities such as Christmas or the Epiphany. In these days, which the Church qualifies as "very holy," [7] it is much less a question of commemorating an event, whose historical reality becomes ever more distant, as it is of reliving, to its very innermost essence, the mystery of which this event was the point of departure, and of reaping the grace peculiar to it. Now the mystery of the Ascension is the mystery of Christ ascending to heaven in order to reign there at the right hand of God and in order to open to us, members of His body, the gates of glory. It is a mystery that is still going on, because it develops in the course of the centuries and will not be completed until the day when the full number of the elect will have corporally joined Christ seated at the heights of the heavens. Therefore is it not evident that, for the very reason of the sublimity of the mystery which constitutes its object, the Ascension of the Lord merits to be celebrated as the most glorious of all the feasts of the liturgical year? Glory, in fact, in the language of Scripture and of Christian tradition is nothing else but the splendor of God precisely as He Himself renders it visible to His creatures. Now there is no mystery where the magnificence of the Divine attributes shines with more brilliance than the one celebrated on Ascension Day. Under whatever aspect we may consider it, it is easy to see this mystery reflect, as does no other, the super-eminent perfection of God.

The Ascension is first of all glorious, it goes without saying, for Christ Himself. In point of fact it is at the moment when the Saviour penetrates heaven in order to be seated there at the right hand of God that the glorification which He solicited from His

Father as the fruit of His own sacrifice is realized: *Et nunc, clarifica me, tu Pater, apud temetipsum, claritate quam habui, priusquam mundus esset, apud te.* "And now do Thou, Father, glorify me with Thyself, with the glory that I had with Thee before the world existed." [8] It was as a consequence of His humility even to death on the cross, St. Paul tells us, that God exalted Christ and gave Him the name that is above all names: *Propter quod et Deus exaltavit illium: et donavit illi nomen quod est super omne nomen.*[9]

Undoubtedly, the Saviour did not wait for the day of His Ascension in order to be invested with His divine glory. From the dawn of His Resurrection, the humanity of Christ was already transformed and His very flesh radiated a heavenly brightness, even though He dissimulated it before the eyes of His disciples, who were unable to withstand its brilliance. But, in order for His glorification to be total and for the working of the divine power in Him to be consummated, it was necessary, in addition, that Christ, the victor over death, raise Himself up to the summit of the heavens so as to introduce His human nature into the place that accorded with its new dignity. This, therefore, is indeed the day in which this human nature took its place on the throne of God, and in which the humanity of Christ completed its change into a divine condition. From the day when He sits at the right hand of His Father, Christ becomes, both as God and as now-glorified man, the equal of Him about Whom, during His mortal life, He could say, "The Father is greater than I," *Pater major me est.*[10] Is it not likewise on the day of the Ascension, when, now finally crowned in heaven, the work accomplished by Christ on earth, from the first moment of the Incarnation, revealed itself as a work in which God Himself had committed His presence and displayed the strength of His arm?

It must be admitted that no other feast of the liturgical year sets the divine transcendence of our Saviour into greater relief than does the solemnity of the Ascension. But we do not think it is useless to point out how present circumstances make opportune, nowadays more than ever before, the celebration of the most glorious of our mysteries. For neither the constant progress of impiety, nor the distressing apostasy of large numbers, nor the furious outburst of infernal powers against the Church must make us forget that, despite deceptive appearances, Christ actually sits at the highest summit of the heavens as a victor over death and as sovereign Master of this world whose destinies He directs. Undoubtedly, ever since the decline of the Middle Ages, Christian piety has been attracted to the sorrowful scenes of the life of the Saviour. There is cause only to rejoice in this, since nothing can quicken our love for Christ like the contemplation of the sufferings that He Himself wished to endure for each one of us. But attention to the sufferings of Christ must not become a detriment to the tribute of adoration and praise which we owe to Him Whom the Church herself ceaselessly invites us to acclaim as "the King of glory," *Rex gloriae*, the sovereign Lord of heaven and earth. Is it not true that the whole liturgical cycle leads back, as if to its center, to the celebration of the paschal mystery, of which the glorious Ascension can be considered as the crown? Reading certain small books of devotion, in which there is more sentimentality than doctrine, one might believe that the Saviour is a defeated person whom we must console for His failures and humiliations. Such a way of presenting things is not only fatal to Christian piety, but is above all contrary to the teaching of the Church herself, which demands that we render homage to Christ as the Eternal Victor, always and everywhere, *semper et ubique Christus vincit, Christus regnat, Christus imperat*. "Christ is victor, Christ rules, Christ commands," such must be the constant affirmation of our Faith.[11]

Glorious for the Son, the feast of the Ascension is no less so for the Father. In fact, Christ petitioned God for His glorification only in order to glorify His Father in Himself: *Pater, venit hora; clarifica Filium Tuum, ut Filius Tuus clarificet Te*.[12] Indeed it is in the glorification of the human nature of the Son of God that we find mirrored with the greatest splendor the boundless wisdom of Him who from all eternity foresaw the fall of human nature, and utilized that very fall for the realization (through the Cross) of that marvelous undertaking — outlined by St. Paul at the beginning of his Epistle to the Ephesians — which reached completion exactly at the moment when the Son of Man, by seating himself on the throne of God, finally united heaven and earth in His own person.[13] As for divine omnipotence, never did the "Father of Glory," *Pater gloriae*, as St. Paul calls Him, manifest it more openly than on the day in which He raised Christ "from the dead, . . . setting Him at His right hand in heaven, above every name, whatever it be, not only in this world, but also in the world to come." [14] By means of the mystery of the Ascension we can likewise know the excess of the charity of God and penetrate the unfathomable abyss of His mercy. For, St. Paul tells us, further on, God "even when we were dead by reason of our sins, brought us to life together with Christ (by grace you have been saved), and raised us up together, and seated us together in heaven in Christ Jesus, that He might show in the ages to come the overflowing riches of His grace in kindness towards us in Christ Jesus." [15]

From all this it must be concluded, with the Apostle himself, that Christ was exalted above the heavens and received the name of "Lord," this name which is above all names and to which all knees bend in heaven, or earth, and under the earth, only in order to glorify, in Himself and by Himself, God the Father, *Quia Dominus Jesus Christus est in gloria Dei Patris.*[16]

For us, frail creatures, the Ascension of the Saviour is the foundation and the certain pledge of our own glorification, as the liturgy proclaims with an eloquent insistence. In the Preface to the Mass, which is probably the work of St. Gregory, the Church gives thanks to God for the fact that Christ rose to heaven, in the sight of His disciples, in order to make us participants in His divinity: *et ipsis cernentibus est elevatus in coelum, ut nos divinitatis suae tribueret esse participes.* On the other hand the Communicantes of the Ascension Mass reminds us, and in very beautiful terms, that the Son of God "has united with our fragile nature in order to place it at the right hand of Divinity," *unitam sibi fragilitatis nostrae substantiam in gloriae suae dextera collocavit.* Thus, our weak humanity, which original sin plunged into an abyss of abjection and subjected to the most humiliating servitude, saw itself, at a single stroke, transported to the height of glory when Christ, ascending above all creatures, took His place at the right hand of the Father. Of course, on the day itself in which the Ascension took place, it was exclusively in the person of the Saviour that human nature shared the glory of Divinity. But, since we are the members of a body of which Christ is the head, why not recognize in our Head's ascension the pledge of our own? St. Leo does not hesitate to proclaim in his noble language, "The ascension of Christ is already ours (*Christi ascensio nostra provectio est*); the glory of the Head lays the foundation of the hope of the body. In this present day (*hodie*) we not only have received assurance of entering into possession of paradise, but, with Christ, we have already penetrated to the heights of the heaven." Because, St. Leo adds, "by incorporating with himself even those whom the ancient enemy snatched from the first abode of felicity, the Son of God has placed them at the right hand of the Father." [17]

Now that He exercises, to our advantage, His sovereign mediation of Pontiff and King, in the celestial sanctuary where He dwells, by virtue of His grace, Christ ceaselessly draws us to Himself, as He had foretold to the Jews during His mortal life: "And I, if I be lifted from the earth, will draw all things to myself," *Et ego, si exaltatus fuero a terra, omnia traham ad meipsum*.[18] This is why the mystery of the Ascension will never be definitively completed until that supreme moment when the last of the elect will have joined Christ in the glory of heaven. This is tantamount to saying that in the glorification of the Saviour we celebrate our own glorification as already realized. From this it follows that the feast of the Ascension, worthily celebrated, must have for a principal effect the renewal and quickening, among all the children of God, of the virtue of Hope, most justly defined as "the soul of Christian life." [19] For, while we wait to join Christ in the abode of glory, Hope, beginning down here below, is the equivalent of the grace of living with Him in the heavens, as the Collect of the day suggests: *Ut ipsi quoque mente in coelestibus habitemus*.

6

The Admirable Ascension

IF THE ASCENSION IS REALLY THE MOST GLORIOUS of all mysteries of the liturgical cycle, it is at the same time the one which most recommends itself to our admiration. For the Ascension is *admirable*, as the Church very justly calls it in the Litany of the Saints. What actually is admiration? No other thing, according to Littré, than "the feeling aroused by what is agreeable or beautiful to the point of astonishment." [1] According to this definition any work must be held to be admirable whose perfection surpasses our expectation because it goes beyond what our mind was capable of conceiving or imagining. Is this not precisely the case with this mystery of the Ascension, whose marvelous breadth and fullness goes infinitely beyond everything we were even in the way of expecting from the wisdom and mercy of God? In fact, is it not at the moment when Christ, our Head, penetrated into heaven in order to introduce our fragile humanity therein that the admirable exchange (*admirabile commercium*) was completed whose humble beginning the liturgy of Christmas allows us to celebrate and to glimpse in its rich consequences? [2] Certainly, it is already an admirable thing that a God make Himself man, but is it not more marvelous and more astonishing still that man, in turn, by virtue of the God-become-man, becomes a sharer of His divinity, *ut nos divinitatis suae triburet esse participes*? Whether it be human or divine, a work seems all the more admirable the higher a perfection it attains.

This is why, from the beginning of the Mass, the antiphon of the Introit very beautifully suggests that we share in the admira-

tion of the disciples gazing up at their beloved Master, who is
going to take His place in heaven in order to introduce us ourselves there one day. *Viri Galilaei, quid admiramini aspicientes
in coelum? Alleluia.* "Men of Galilee, what then are you admiring
gazing up at the sky?" [3] Moreover, the Church herself, on this day
as glorious for her as it is for our Saviour, does not seem to be
able to take her eyes off the spectacle that she contemplates with
rapture. From one end of the Office to the other, in the hymns and
in the responses, in the antiphons and in the versicles, she never
tires of expressing, with a vibrant enthusiasm, the admiration that
the triumph of the royal Bridegroom inspires in her, and whose
glory she already shares here below. Often, like the Psalmist,
whose language requires a new freshness on her lips, the Church
addresses herself directly to the Saviour. Sometimes she proclaims
His magnificence, which from now on shines forth in the heights
of heaven; [4] sometimes she salutes Him rising on the celestial
clouds, as on a chariot, and borne on the wings of the wind, as
He climbs upward clothed in majesty and splendor, enveloped in
light as in a garment; [5] sometimes she exhorts Him to display His
divine vigor so that she may still further exalt His power and
strength.[6]

At certain moments, the Church is as if dazzled by the brilliance
of the spectacle that she contemplates. Then she expresses her
admiration in small, short, rapid phrases, regularly broken by a
joyous Alleluia: "The Lord is in His holy temple, the Lord is in
heaven, Alleluia!" [7] "He is risen, Alleluia, infinitely higher than
all the angels, Alleluia!" [8] "The Lord is in Sinai, Alleluia; He is
great, He is sublime, Alleluia!"; [9] "The Lord is in heaven, Alleluia! He has prepared His throne, Alleluia!" [10]

But it is above all by appropriating the 46th Psalm, which is
pre-eminently the Psalm of the Ascension, that the Church en-
treats all nations to join her in order to clap their hands and
exhalt the Son of God by hymns of praise and jubilation:

> O clap your hands, all ye nations:
> Shout unto God with the voice of joy,
> For the Lord is high, terrible;

A great king over all the earth.
God is ascended with jubilee,
And the Lord with the sound of the trumpet.
Sing praises to our king, sing ye.
For God is the king of all the earth,
Sing ye wisely.
God shall reign over the nations,
God sitteth on His holy throne.[11]

Do we wish to gather the superabundant riches of grace that the Ascension of the Lord reserves for all those who strive to live this mystery liturgically? Then let us know how to respond to the pressing invitation that the Church makes to us to join her in her praise in order to offer God the homage of our thankfulness and of our joy.

7

The Joyous Ascension

Of all the mysteries of christ the ascension is certainly the one that manifests itself as the most glorious, the one which the Church herself considers as the most admirable. But why not recognize that the Ascension is likewise one of the most joyous mysteries of our liturgical year? How could the return of the Saviour to heaven, where He sits forever at the right hand of God and where, on our behalf, He exercises His royal mediation, give rise to any other feeling in our hearts than one of a very keen and pure joy? There are those who say, it is true, that upon leaving the earth the Lord removed Himself from His disciples' sight and that He likewise deprived us of His visible presence until the end of time. Not infrequently the Apostles, after the Ascension, are pictured as being "at once deeply grieved over the departure of the Master and joyous over His triumph." [1] But we have only to refer to that passage in the Gospel where St. Luke recounts the scene of the Ascension to ascertain that such a way of interpreting the attitude of the Apostles rests on no foundation. In fact, after telling us that Jesus had gone with His disciples towards Bethany, the Evangelist adds, "He lifted up His hands and blessed them. And it came to pass as He blessed them that He parted from them and was carried up into heaven. And they worshipped Him, and returned to Jerusalem with great joy (*cum gaudio magno*). And they were continually in the temple, praising and blessing God." [2] Thus, there was no question at all of pain or regret among the disciples. Besides, why should anyone wish that the return of the Saviour to the Father should cause some sadness among those of His company?

First of all it must be clearly pointed out that the separation of the Master from His disciples, the effective and truly painful separation, took place at the moment of the Passion. When Christ was delivered to the Jews, condemned to death, crucified and buried, it was the occasion of a very bitter disappointment, and not only for the disciples but for all those who had hoped in Him. Nothing is more significant in this regard than the state of mind of those two disciples who walked so sadly along the road to Emmaus, on the very evening of the Resurrection. To Jesus, who had joined them in the guise of a stranger and had asked them the cause of their sadness, they replied that all their hopes had come to naught because the person from whom they had expected the redemption of Israel had just been condemned to death and crucified.

Undoubtedly the Apostles saw their Master again after the Resurrection, but in conditions that were not at all the same as formerly. The risen Christ was no longer of the earth, no longer lived in the society of His disciples. He did not manifest His mysterious presence to them except in a certain number of apparitions, several of which are recounted in the Gospel, apparitions, more or less rapid but always transitory, whose aim was to convince the Apostles of the reality of the Resurrection and to prepare them for the advent of the Paraclete. Finally the Apostles, St. Leo tells us, had acquired such a faith in the Resurrection of the Saviour that His return to heaven, far from causing them the least sadness, filled them with an immense joy: *Ita sunt veritate perspicua roborati, ut Domino in coelorum eunte sublimia, non solum nulla afficerentur tristitia, sed etiam magno gaudio replerentur.*[3]

After the Ascension the disciples returned to Jerusalem, their souls filled with a great gladness, not only because they were definitely certain of the triumph of their Master, but because He had promised not to leave them orphans but to return to them spiritually in the Person of the Paraclete.[4] They had at last understood the words of the Saviour, "It is expedient for you that I depart. For if I do not go the Advocate (Paraclete) will not come to you; but if I go I will send him to you." Far from expressing regret at their Master's departure, the disciples gathered in the temple to bless God, to give Him thanks for the marvels to which they had been witnesses and which they would soon have the happiness of making known to the world.

If, therefore, the Ascension was an occasion of great joy for the disciples of the Saviour, and of an unmixed joy, why does not the liturgical celebration of this same mystery fill us also with a similar gladness? Furthermore, we have already seen that the liturgy of the feast expresses only a very serene and very pure joy, a joy veiled by no cloud of sadness or regret. The Church never ceases to repeat, *Jubilate Deo in voce exsultationis,* "Sing aloud to God in joyful voice." The joy of the Ascension is not reserved to the inhabitants of heaven, to the angels and the elect, but must be shared by all those who still remain on earth. More, given the close bond that unites the two mysteries, is not the Ascension, for us also, the prelude to Pentecost? Not only does the triumphal return of Christ to His Father renew among all the children of God the hope of their complete glorification, not only does it invite them to fix their hearts where their real joys dwell, but it prepares them to receive shortly this unstinted pouring out of the Holy Ghost, which will mark the completion of the paschal solemnities.

St. Leo, who always so deeply penetrates into the spirit of the mysteries which he tells us about, recommends that we celebrate the Ascension in joy and thanksgiving. "Since," he says, "the Ascension of Christ is also ours and the glory of the Head lays the foundation of the hope of the body, let us exult, beloved brethren, in the feelings of a just happiness, and let us rejoice in a fervent thanksgiving, *Dignis, dilectissimi exultemus gaudiis, et pia gratiarum actione laetemur.*" [5]

8

The Ascension, Prelude to Pentecost

AT FIRST THE ASCENSION OF THE SAVIOUR WAS celebrated at the same time as the descent of the Holy Ghost upon the apostles, that is to say on the last day of the fifty-day paschal period. In fact during the first three centuries there is not the slightest trace of a feast of the Ascension celebrated on the fortieth day of Easter. The famous Spanish pilgrim Etheria, in her account of her travels, informs us that the church in Jerusalem, as late as the 4th century, solemnly memorialized the Ascension on the same day when the feast of Pentecost was celebrated. After having commemorated the descent of the Holy Ghost upon the disciples in the morning of this day, and at Tierce, in the sanctuary constructed on the site of the Cenacle, the worshipers, according to Etheria, went to the Mount of Olives, to Imbomon, "that is to say to the place from where the Lord rose to heaven; and there the bishop sits down, readings are given, interspersed with hymns and antiphons appropriate to the day and place, and the Gospel passage is read which speaks of the Ascension of the Lord into the heavens after His Resurrection." [1] There certainly was, it is true, a celebration of the night office and the Mass in the Church of Bethlehem on the fortieth day after Easter, but in this circumstance, again according to Etheria's testimony, no reference was made to the Ascension of the Lord. The sermon, suited to the day and the place, could have no other subject but the Nativity of Christ. According to the historian Eusebius of Caesarea, the Ascension and Pentecost were celebrated simultaneously on the fiftieth day after Easter. It is on this day, says Eusebius, "the last of the whole series, the one which it would not be at all wrong to

31

call the feast of feasts (*omnium festivitatum maxima*), towards the
hour of afternoon that he (Constantine) departed towards the
Lord." [2] Hence, Eusebius calls the last day of the fifty-day paschal
period "the wholly festive day of the Ascension (ἀναλήψεως) of
Christ." [3] St. Ambrose also seems to unite the Ascension and Pentecost in the same festivity.[4] It is necessary to come up as far as the
end of the fourth century in order to find the first positive evidence attesting that the feast of the Ascension was definitely
separated from Pentecost, and celebrated on the fortieth day.[5]

This persistence in not wishing to celebrate the Ascension on
the fiftieth day, at the same time as Pentecost, should not surprise
us. It is easily explainable. First, it did not seem possible to celebrate the Ascension on its proper date without its being to the
detriment of the number fifty, which symbolizes the fullness of the
paschal time. Was not Pentecost considered as the day in which
the grace of the fifty-day period radiated to its fullest extent? To
celebrate the Ascension on the fortieth day, in some way, was
like breaking the mysterious unity of the fifty-day paschal period.
Undoubtedly this was the reason for the canon of the Council of
Elvira, held around 400, forbidding the solemnization of the
fortieth day after Easter, and the closing of the paschal period on
this date.[6] Moreover, the ancients, and justly so, considered the
two mysteries of the Ascension and Pentecost as absolutely in-
separable, since Christ had ascended to heaven only in order to
have the Holy Ghost descend. The Saviour Himself had said to
His disciples, "It is expedient for you that I depart. For if I do
not go, the Advocate (Paraclete) will not come to you; but if I
go, I will send him to you." [7] On the very day of Pentecost, Saint
Peter himself also testified before the Jews of the link that ties
the two mysteries to each other. "This Jesus," he told them, "God
has raised up, and we are all witnesses of it. Therefore, exalted by
the right hand of God, and receiving from the Father the promise
of the Holy Spirit, he hath poured forth the Spirit which you see
and hear." [8]

If the glorification of Christ was definitively completed when
He ascended to heaven in order to sit there at the right hand of
God, it was still necessary for the Holy Ghost to descend here
below in order to manifest this glory and in order Himself to be

the unimpeachable and permanent witness to it, until the end of time. "The exaltation of Christ and the descent of the Holy Ghost," writes Dom Vonier, "are one and the same mystery, one and the same fact, because the Holy Ghost is the very Spirit of Christ seated at the right hand of the Father." [9]

PART TWO

The Solemnity of Pentecost

9

The Sunday before Pentecost,
The Witness of the Paraclete,
And of the Disciples

Before the feast of the ascension was given an Octave, the Sunday which in our missal is entitled *Dominica infra octavem Ascensionis*, "Sunday in the Octave of the Ascension," was called *Dominica I*a *post Ascensionem*, "First Sunday after Ascension." [1]

In the Middle Ages a stational Mass was celebrated on this day in the Pantheon of Agrippa, which Pope Boniface IV at the beginning of the 7th century had transformed into a Christian basilica under the title Saint Mary of the Martyrs.[2] Situated between the Ascension and Pentecost, this Sunday owes the character peculiar to it to its place, because it differs obviously in its liturgical key from the three Sundays that precede it.

It is not surprising that the Mass of a Sunday that follows the Ascension should reflect the influence of the latter mystery. The antiphon of the Introit expresses the intense desire felt by the Church to see again the radiant countenance of this *Rex pacificus*, Whose marvelous beauty was already sung in the Christmas liturgy and Who, upon ascending to heaven, has disappeared from our bodily eyes.

> Hear, O Lord, my voice,
>   With which I have cried to thee;
> My heart hath said to thee:
> My face has sought thee:

Turn not away thy face from me.
Alleluia, Alleluia![3]

For as long as the Lord remained visible here below, by virtue
of His Incarnation, we have sought and followed Him in each
of the mysteries that we have been able to relive with the Church,
from His birth on Christmas night up to His glorious Ascension.
Now that He has ascended to heaven we must still seek Him with
perserverance until it becomes possible for us to join Him in the
abode of His glory and there to contemplate the uncovered splendor of His countenance.

Anticipating the realization of our supreme hope, and in order
to maintain in us the joy of the Ascension, the first alleluiatic
versicle of the Mass proclaims that the Saviour has left this world
only to sit on the throne of divinity and to reign there in all
eternity over all the nations of the earth:

> *Regnavit Dominus super omnes gentes;*
> *Deus sedet super sedem sanctam suam.*[4]

Moreover, the antiphon of the Offertory, which is exactly the
same as that of the Ascension, reminds us once more that the
return of the Lord to the Father was carried out in jubilation and
to the joyous sound of celestial trumpets:

> *Ascendit Deus in jubilatione*
> *Et Dominus in voce tubae.*[5]

More than the mystery of the Ascension, however, it is the
mystery of Pentecost which dominates the liturgy of this Sunday,
the Gospel of which gives us a presentiment of the pouring out of
the Holy Ghost.[6] In fact in the passage from St. John read at the
Mass of the last Sunday preceding Pentecost, Our Lord an-
nounces to His disciples that He will send them the Paraclete with
the mission of bearing witness to Him before all the world. But,
by virtue of this same Paraclete, the disciples themselves will also
have to bear witness to their Master:

"But when the Advocate (Paraclete) has come, whom I will
send you from the Father, the Spirit of Truth who proceeds from
the Father, he will bear witness concerning me. And you also will
bear witness, because from the beginning you are with me."[7]

In order to grasp clearly the import of these words and the practical conclusion which derives therefrom in the thinking of the Church, we must recall that we are coming to the end of the fifty-day period. During the preceding weeks, the neophytes of the paschal night have strengthened themselves in their Faith and have had the leisure to develop the grace received and to render it fruitful. The remainder of the faithful have been able, for their part, to profit from these same weeks in order to renew themselves profoundly in their baptismal lives and to undertake a more resolute practice of their Christian Faith. The abundant pouring out of the Holy Ghost which will be effected on the day of Pentecost will have the result of completing the work of the risen Christ throughout the entire Mystical Body and of completing that Easter renewal.

But after Pentecost the Church will resume her march towards eternity under the usual conditions. During the long period that is to follow, that is to say, until the next Easter, all Christians, the formerly and the newly baptized, will have to make use of the graces received during the fifty-day paschal period. Like the Apostles, they will have to fight and struggle to bear witness of their Faith to Christ, because the malice of men has persecutions and ordeals of all kinds in store for them. Before dying, the Master had not concealed from His disciples all that they would have to suffer from the world because of Him:

"They will expel you from the synagogues. Yes, the hour is coming for anyone who kills you to think that he is offering worship to God. And these things they will do because they have not known the Father nor me. But these things I have spoken to you, that when the time for them has come you may remember that I told you." [8]

Does not this warning of the Lord continue to be very valid in modern times? Is it not opportune, in these final days of the Easter time, to recall — not only to the newly baptized but to all Christians — that the new pouring out of the Holy Ghost which they will receive on the day of Pentecost will have the aim of fortifying them and making them capable of being witnesses to Christ before the whole world, without fearing either the malevolence of unbelievers or the hostility of the impious? They will have nothing to fear since it is the Holy Ghost, the Spirit of Christ, who will live, act and bear witness in them.

Moreover, in the prayer which He said after the Last Supper for His very own disciples, the prayer called "priestly," the Saviour includes all those who will continue to bear witness to Him until the end of time. Now the Church, in the antiphon of the Communion, specifically recalls to God the petition which Christ formerly addressed Him on behalf of all His disciples:

"While I was with them, I kept them in thy name. Those whom thou hast given me I guarded. But now that I am coming to thee, I do not pray that thou take them out of the world, but that thou keep them from evil (*sed ut serves eos a malo*), alleluia! alleluia!" [9]

Already in the Psalm of the Introit (of which only the first verse remains today, but the greater part of which doubtless would normally have been sung) Christians who hasten to bear witness affirm their absolute trust in divine protection:

> The Lord is my light and my salvation;
>> Whom then should I fear?
> The Lord is the protector of my life;
>> Of whom should I be afraid?
> Though an army should encamp against me,
>> My heart shall not fear.
> Though a war rise against me,
>> Even then shall I have trust.

Finally, according to the Secret prayer of the Mass, the Church, on this last Sunday preceding Pentecost, rightly offers the Sacrifice so that the Saviour may purify His disciples through the virtue of the Eucharist, and fortify them through the strength of celestial grace:

Sacrificia nos, Domine, immaculata purificent, et mentibus nostris supernae gratiae dent vigorem.[10]

The surest sign that the spirit of Christ, the Paraclete, acts inside the souls of those of whom it takes hold, evidently is the persistent practice of fraternal Charity, as the Epistle of the Mass recalls:

"But above all things" — declares St. Peter, whose words the

Church appropriates here — "have a constant mutual charity among yourselves." [11]

To be sure, this fraternal charity must be effective and sustained. Therefore it is necessary that each one make the community of which he is a member benefit from the spiritual riches which the Holy Ghost will dispense to each one, in various degrees, in this solemnity of Pentecost, on which all the paschal work will reach completion.

"Be hospitable to one another without murmuring," — says the Chief of the Apostles further — "according to the gift that each has received; administer it to one another as good stewards of the manifold grace of God. If anyone speaks, let it be as with the words of God. If anyone ministers, let it be as from the strength that God furnishes; that in all things God may be honored through Jesus Christ, to whom are the glory and dominion forever." [12]

What the Church asks of Christians who are preparing themselves shortly to receive a new pouring out of the Holy Ghost, we shall find properly realized on the morrow of the first Pentecost, in that community at Jerusalem of which it is said that the members were of but one heart and soul: *cor unum et anima una.*[13]

In fact, no witness could be more eloquent and decisive in the eyes of the world than that of a Christian community whose members, united in fraternal Charity, seek nothing else in the exercise of their respective functions than the glory of God. Moreover, did not the Master Himself say to His disciples, "By this will all men know that you are my disciples, if you have love for one another." [14]

In order that Christians may be able to bear the witness they owe to Christ, their will must be totally subjected to Him whom they recognize as the Lord, and they must be capable of serving Him with perfect purity of heart. The Church is aware of this when she petitions God that our wills be ever subject to Him and that we serve Him with a truly pure heart: *Omnipotens sempiterne Deus, fac nos tibi semper et devotam gerere voluntatem et Majestati tuae sincero corde servire.*[15] The grace which this beautiful Collect of the Sunday solicits is nothing else but the grace

of true devotion, that is to say of devotion in the sense that the
liturgy gives this word. For it is superfluous to point out that devotion, as the Church understands it here, does not rest in the sensi-
bility, but in the will. Devotion, writes Dom Marmion, "is the
most delicate flower and the most pure fruit of love, because it is
love impelled to the gift, to the total sacrifice of self to the beloved
being." [16] Thus understood, devotion can be considered the funda-
mental disposition of all Christian life, for every Christian, by
virtue of his baptism, is entirely consecrated to God, consecrated
in his heart and even in the body, the latter becoming, according
to St. Paul, the temple of the Holy Ghost.[17] Now Christian life
consists precisely in recognizing that we belong completely to God
and in responding effectively to this awareness in the exercise of
all our activity, but first of all and above all, in giving to the Lord,
with a fervent heart, the devotion due to Him. Faith and devotion
are the two dispositions to which the Church, in the course of her
Eucharistic prayer, directs the attention of the Lord in recom-
mending those who are participating in the Sacrifice of the Mass.[18]
Therefore, would it be possible for the formerly and newly baptized to arrive at the end of the fifty-day paschal period without
offering Christ the witness of a more ardent faith, and of a more
complete and sustained devotion?

A few more days still and the paschal time will be over. No
other liturgical period will have been more quickening and fecund
than this one. The feast of Easter has gained for many Christians
the privilege of being born to the life of the risen Christ. It has
allowed a still greater number of other souls to emerge from the
shadows of sin and to recover light and peace. For all Christians
it was the opportunity to participate in the redemptive mystery
and to relive the successive phases through the liturgy. During the
fifty paschal days prayers and hymns are the expression of our
keen and very joyous gratitude towards Him from whom so many
blessings flow.[19] But, so that these dispositions of gratitude may
not be simply ephemeral, the Postcommunion of this last Sunday
before the great pouring out of Pentecost petitions God, and very
rightly, to let us remain in a perpetual thanksgiving, "*Ut in grati-
arium semper actione maneamus.*" It goes without saying that it

is a question of giving thanks not only by expressing them in our prayers, but by doing all things "so that God is glorified through Jesus Christ our Lord." *Ut in omnibus honorifectur Deus per Jesum Christum Dominun nostrum.*[20] Nothing does greater honor to God than thanksgiving. Was not it the first witness that the Apostles would bear Him publicly on the very day of Pentecost when, after having received the Holy Ghost, they left the Cenacle proclaiming the *Magnalia Dei?*

Pentecost, the Mystery of Christ

EVEN THOUGH IT IS PERSONAL TO THE HOLY Ghost, we must no less consider the coming of Pentecost as a mystery of Christ, the mystery upon which the work of Redemption is completed. Undoubtedly Christian piety rightly sees in the solemnity of Pentecost the great liturgical feast of the third Person of the Holy Trinity, which is manifested with such brilliance on this day. But neither must such piety forget that in this circumstance the Church celebrates the coming of the Holy Ghost as the necessary crown, the indispensable completion of a work which remains, in all its parts and according to its diverse aspects, the glorious work of the immolated and risen Christ.

That Pentecost constitutes an integrating part of this paschal mystery of which the death and Resurrection of the Saviour, followed by His Ascension, form as it were the first stages — all this is evident, for without the pouring out of the Holy Ghost on the fiftieth day after Easter the work of our salvation would be incomplete, ineffective. It is true that through His Resurrection Christ had already given life to our human nature, and that through His Ascension "He placed the fragility of our substance at the right hand of God." [1] But, the triumph of life over death being exclusively realized in the person of our Head, it was all the more necessary that the new life be transmitted from Christ, who had fullness of it for us, to the whole of the Mystical Body, to the members of the ransomed and forgiven human race. For the right is not the fact, and, although regenerated in right, humanity could not live in fact the life of the risen Christ until it had been effectively transmitted to them.

The messianic era had, by the prophets, been awaited as reserving a large and abundant pouring out of the Spirit of the Lord. The liturgy of the Pentecost, of course, does not neglect to remind us of this promise that God had made to His people. "And I will give you a new heart, and put a new spirit within you." [2]

On the very day of Pentecost, St. Peter before the Jews attests that the realization of what had been predicted by the prophet Joel has already commenced. "And it shall come to pass after this, that I will pour out my spirit upon all flesh: and your sons and daughters shall prophesy: your old men shall dream dreams, and your young men shall see visions. Moreover upon my servants and handmaids on those days I will pour forth my spirit." [3]

Now it was upon Christ Himself that the care devolved of spreading abroad on earth that Spirit of God of which He had to possess the plenitude. St. John the Baptist hints plainly at the essential difference that separates His own mission from that of the Redeemer when he declares to the Jews: "I have baptized you with water, but he will baptize you with the Holy Spirit." [4] In fact, in the course of a conversation which preceded the Ascension, the Saviour recommended to His disciples that they not leave Jerusalem before the fulfillment of the promise of the Father, "for," he said, "John indeed baptized with water, but you shall be baptized with the Holy Spirit not many days hence." [5]

Everything that Christ accomplished in the course of His earthly mission was ordained for the fulfillment of the divine promise. If the mortal life of the Saviour was completely oriented towards the hour of His passion, "His hour," it is precisely because the sacrifice of the Cross was indispensable for the sending from on high of the Spirit who was to be the principle of a new life for us, the life of the resurrected Christ. By His teaching, under all the diverse forms it took, Christ was leading up to the pouring out of the Holy Ghost in revealing to souls the conditions of the kingdom that He had come to inaugurate on earth — its spiritual character and high moral requirements. The prayer of the Son of God become man never had any other object, directly or indirectly, than that of the sending of the Paraclete. Of this the first petitions of the Our Father provide manifest proof, for the hallowing of the Divine Name, the coming of the kingdom, the fulfillment of the will of the Lord on earth as in heaven – all this could be realized only in the Church, and only through the permanent activity of the Holy Ghost dwelling in her. In that priestly prayer which He pronounces before dying and in which He expresses to His Father His supreme desire, the Saviour petitions for the members of His Mystical Body, and as the fruit of His own Sacrifice, that absolute unity which requires among all Christians the presence of a common Spirit, the Spirit who proceeds from the Father and the Son. In all His activity here below, His examples and His works, His sermons and miracles, Christ never had any other aim but the glorification of His Father. But for this it was necessary that He Himself be glorified in the Church precisely as that Church is anointed and governed by the Spirit of God.

Not only did Christ through His preaching prepare souls for the great pouring out of Pentecost, not only did He petition it from God in His prayer and obtain it through the merits of His Cross, but it was He Himself who, once lifted up into the glory of heaven, received from His Father the mission of pouring forth the Holy Ghost, His Spirit, upon His own disciples. In a last conversation with the latter, the Saviour had announced, "It is expedient for you that I depart. For if I do not go, the Advocate (Paraclete) will not come to you, but if I go, I will send him to you. (Si autem abiero, mittam eum ad vos)" [6]

In fact, on the day of Pentecost, it is to Christ Himself as its author that St. Peter directly attributes the pouring out of the Holy Ghost, the marvelous effects of which aroused so great an excitement in Jerusalem. "Therefore, exalted by the right hand of God, and receiving from the Father the promise of the Holy Spirit, he has poured forth this Spirit which you see and hear." [7]

In this precious text, St. Peter, chief of the Apostles, presents to us the pouring out of the Holy Ghost as the work of the Saviour Himself and as the immediate consequence of His glorification. In fact, from the day on which the Holy Ghost made Himself present in the Church in order to act in her, He becomes the living and permanent witness of the glorification of Christ Jesus.

Perhaps no one has shed light on this truth more felicitously than has Dom Vonier in a remarkable chapter of his beautiful book, *The Victory of Christ*, in which he expresses himself as follows:

"The descent of the Holy Ghost on the fiftieth day after the Resurrection of Christ is the official proclamation made by God Himself of the supreme victory of Christ. The Apostles considered it as the outer manifestation of the hidden victory of Christ, and it is thus it must be considered by us. The Holy Ghost is the herald of this victory; His mission is to glorify Christ: 'He will glorify me, because he will receive of what is mine and declare it to you.'

"This very special coming of the Third Person of the Holy Trinity, of the Holy Ghost, which took place on the first Pentecost, is essentially linked to the great victory of Christ. The Spirit Himself, as He appeared then, is a Spirit of victory. We have seen the Son of God achieve victory, but on this earth He has never assumed the glories of this triumph. This triumph became the office of the Holy Ghost on the day of this special manifestation — different from the other comings of the Spirit — which is called Pentecost, and which is evidently a permanent revelation. Up to the end of days, the triumph of Jesus is personified in a Divine Person. The Holy Ghost among us, as at Pentecost, is the outer proclamation of all the hidden exploits of the divine Hero, Jesus Christ." [8]

The Holy Ghost is, as Dom Vonier calls Him, the "glorifier" of Christ. "The glory of Our Lord here below, therefore, is much more than the memory preserved by believers of all that He is and of all that He had done; his glory is a Divine Person." Thus there is no ground to fear that the glory of the Saviour may ever suffer the slightest diminution in this world.

Since His coming the Holy Ghost does not cease to bear witness to Christ in the Church, because the mystery of Pentecost — as we shall see later — develops and comes to bloom in the Church. The glorification of Christ continues here below through the growth of His Mystical Body and the continual sanctification of its members, which is specifically the work of the Holy Ghost, whose activity never slackens, even during periods of history which strike us as darkest, and most desolating. There is not a light, not a grace which has not been acquired for us by the merits of Christ and which we do not owe to the working of His Spirit. This is not to

say that the Paraclete came into this world to supplant Christ, to
substitute for Him or to take His place. "Nothing would be more
false than such an explanation of His mission. He is not even a
power which succeeds another power, as though Jesus had accomplished His part of the work of Redemption and then had
returned to the Father, leaving the Holy Ghost to complete the
work. No, the Spirit who came on earth has come with all the
fragrance of the Incarnation on His wings. The Redemption is
not a discontinuous work. Jesus accomplished it completely; nobody has succeeded Him. The only change is that His interior
Presence replaces His exterior Presence. Christ invisible, the Holy
Ghost who had been hidden in Christ all the time, now governs the
Church and governs it with an energy, with an efficiency which
still render Him almost palpable and exterior, for the characteristic of this Epiphany of the Holy Ghost, begun at Pentecost, is
that the Holy Ghost speaks and acts manifestly and that His works
are visible." [9]

Before leaving His disciples and dying, the Lord had promised
them that He would not leave them orphans and that He would
come back to them: *Non relinquam vos orphanos*.[10] After His
resurrection, the Lord had given them assurance that He would
be with them until the consummation of the world: *Ecce ego
vobiscum omnibus diebus usque ad consummationen saeculi*.[11]
Christ made real His promise on the day of Pentecost by sending
down the Paraclete who was to assure His invisible presence here
below, until the moment when He Himself would reappear on the
clouds of heaven in all the brilliance of His divine glory.[12]

II

The Epiphany of the Paraclete:
Christmas and Pentecost
Note on the Introit "Spiritus Domini"

Nothing could take place under more humble conditions and in a more silent way than the coming of the Word according to the flesh. In order to clothe Himself in our fragile nature in the condition in which the fall of the first man had left it, the Son of God elected to descend into the womb of a young virgin who lived in retirement in the obscure village of Nazareth. The divine operation was effected in the greatest secrecy, and St. Joseph himself was advised of it only later by a celestial messenger. Christ remained enclosed for nine months in the womb of His Mother. Then, at the end of this long retreat, He came into the world in the middle of the profound silence of the night, *dum medium silentium tenerent omnia.*[1] His virginal birth in a poor crib had no witnesses save the angels from heaven. No one was informed of the coming of the King of Kings save the humble shepherds who were guarding their flocks near Bethlehem, and, a little later, a few Magi from the distant East who were discreetly informed by the silent language of a star. Begun under such conditions, the coming of the Saviour was the starting point of a life passed entirely in a little corner of Palestine, in poverty and labor, before ending painfully on Calvary in extreme abjection.

What a contrast between this obscure event on Christmas day, and the one which took place some thirty years later on a certain day of Pentecost under the extraordinary circumstances reported in the Acts of the Apostles! [2]

Hardly had the Saviour ascended into heaven when in obedience to their Master the Apostles returned to Jerusalem. There they retired into a private dwelling, undoubtedly in that same Cenacle where they had celebrated Passover and where Jesus manifested Himself several times after His Resurrection. It was there that for more than a week the Apostles, who had been joined by a certain number of disciples and several pious women, among whom was the Mother of the Lord, in persevering prayer together prepared themselves to receive the Paraclete promised by Christ.[3] Now on the fiftieth day after the Resurrection of the Saviour, as they were gathered in the Cenacle, there suddenly came a sound from heaven like a violent wind which swept through the whole house, causing it to shake noisily. At the same moment there appeared a globe of fire which divided into flames each of which settled on each one of those present. They were filled with the Holy Ghost and they began to speak in unknown tongues, according as the Holy Ghost prompted them to speak. At the hour when this prodigious event took place, a great multitude of pilgrims, come from "every nation under heaven," was gathered in Jerusalem to celebrate the Jewish feast of the First Fruits. There were Parthians, Medes, Elamites, and inhabitants of Mesopotamia, Judea, and Cappadoccia, Pontus and Asia, Phyrgea, Pamphylia, Egypt and parts of Libya about Cyrene. And there were also visitors from Rome, Jews as well as proselytes, Cretans and Arabians. Upon hearing this unusual noise that came from the Cenacle, the amazed multitude ran towards the place of the prodigy. But when each one heard, in his own language, the disciples of Christ (for the most part Galileans) praising the wonderful works of God, there was general stupefaction.[4]

However, some hardy souls having taken advantage of the occasion to make fun of the Apostles and accuse them of being drunk with "new wine," St. Peter judged that the hour had come to speak up in order to shed light on the true import of the event which had aroused such an emotion in a religious city. He showed how the pouring out of the Holy Ghost, of which all had perceived the marvelous effects, was the work of the very Jesus whom the Jews had crucified, but whom God had raised up and placed at His right hand.

The liturgy of Pentecost will happily set into relief the extraordinary brilliance that surrounded this coming of the Holy Ghost, which offers so striking a contrast with that other coming on Christmas night in the silence and poverty of Bethlehem. Many texts of the Office and the Mass repeatedly remind us of the extraordinary phenomena which rendered the coming of the Paraclete manifest to all.[5] Even a passage as habitually sober as the Communicantes of the Canon of the Mass will stress as characterizing the very holy day of Pentecost the apparition of the tongues of fire.[6]

Nor will the liturgy fail to shed full light on the complete dimension of the coming which inaugurates the universal phase of the kingdom which Christ came to establish here below. For the nascent Church was not to be confined for long within the precincts of Jerusalem. Under the influence of the Holy Ghost, Apostles and disciples were to leave the Cenacle only to spread the Gospel over the entire surface of the world. This is precisely what is affirmed by the Introit *Spiritus Domini*, which with the impetus of a keen enthusiasm and an admirable vigor magnificently opens the Mass and, we think, can be translated as follows:

> The Spirit of the Lord has filled the universe, alleluia,
> And even that which contains all things
> Now has (habet) the knowledge of praise; alleluia,
> alleluia, alleluia.[7]

12

The Fiftieth Day

AMONG THE CHRISTIAN WRITERS OF THE FIRST three centuries the term Pentecost ($\pi\epsilon\nu\tau\eta\kappa o\sigma\tau\acute{\eta}$) designates the period that begins with the Resurrection of the Saviour and terminates exactly fifty days later. Such is, perhaps, the meaning of the term of this word in the books of the Acts.[1] At any rate for Tertullian the *Pentecostes* is nothing else but the joyous interval (*laetissimum spatium*) of fifty days during which the Church simultaneously celebrates the three glorious mysteries in the Resurrection, the Ascension, and the descent of the Holy Ghost.[2] But, the realization of this latter mystery having taken place on the same day in which the fifty-day paschal period ends, it became customary to make a more special commemoration of the fiftieth day, which thereby became our feast of Pentecost.[3] However, this particular commemoration of the fiftieth day was further reduced to a matter of small importance in the 3rd century, since the Council of Elvira in 300 had to insist on the obligation to celebrate it.[4]

It was not before the middle of the 4th century that the feast of Pentecost, in the East as well as the West, received all the liturgical development which was fitting to the celebration of the great mystery of which it is the subject.

The place held in the work of Redemption by the capital occurrence, of which each feast of Pentecost is the anniversary, already would suffice to justify the importance that we must attach to its celebration. But we must repeat here what we said before with regard to the mystery of the Ascension. Pentecost is something else, and much more, than a simple anniversary, the anniversary of this pouring out of the Holy Ghost which took place in Jerusalem in marvelous circumstances, several days after the glorification of Christ, and for the Church marked the point of departure of her apostolic activity.

On the one hand, in fact, Pentecost is but the fulfillment and the conclusion of the paschal solemnities. Pentecost, as St. Augustine said, is the solemnity of Easter come to its end without losing aught of its brilliance. If Easter is the beginning of grace, Pentecost is its crown. In calling Pentecost "the center of all the solemnities" [5] St. John Chrysostom "does not claim that the feast of the fiftieth day raises it above that of Easter, but would have us understand that it occupies, so to speak, the summit of the paschal mystery, and is its supreme and definitive flowering. Moreover, the ancient Roman liturgy also stressed, in more than one Collect, that the feast of Pentecost completes and summarizes the whole mystery of Easter. "O Almighty and eternal God," reads a Collect of the Leonine Sacramentary, "Thou who hast wished to enclose all our Easter in this mysterious fiftieth day." [6] At Easter we celebrate Christ's victory over sin and over death, but at Pentecost we celebrate, with the ultimate consequence of His victory, the fullness of His triumph.

On the other hand, the feast of the fiftieth day completes the paschal mystery only to inaugurate a new mystery, because upon the coming of the Paraclete there begins that great mystery of Pentecost, which, by continuing in the life of the Church, will never cease to develop and to extend until the end of time. Since He has descended upon the earth, not only does the Holy Ghost sanctify and govern in its totality this Body of Christ of which Christians are the living members, but, ever more, every year, on the same day when the Church celebrates the mystery of Pentecost, he brings about normally, in all souls who have been able to relive faithfully the paschal solemnities, something similar to what long ago he accomplished with such brilliance in each of the disciples gathered at the Cenacle in Jerusalem.

13

The First Pentecost

IN ORDER TO FORM AN EXACT IDEA OF WHAT IS renewed every year in the Church in the feast of Pentecost, it is indispensable to recall what happened in Jerusalem when, after the Ascension of the Saviour and in conformity to His promise, the Holy Ghost spread Himself over His apostles and His disciples. At the very moment when the Paraclete descended on the Cenacle, something like tongues of fire appeared which separated and settled on each one of the persons present. Fire was the symbol chosen by the Holy Ghost to manifest His invisible action in the souls. Now the special quality of fire is to illuminate the places which it penetrates, with its light, but also to consume through its ardor everything that it is capable of reaching and enkindling. Well, what the virtue of fire produced materially, the activity of the Holy Ghost realized spiritually in each one of the numerous disciples gathered in the Cenacle.

It is beyond doubt that, up to the coming of the Paraclete, the disciples of Christ and the Apostles themselves had only a very imperfect knowledge of their Master. Although they had been instructed by Christ and trained by Him, although they had been witnesses of His miracles, although they had been able to live long months in intimacy with him and gather the last outpourings of His heart at the Cenacle, the disciples still remained strangers to the thought of the Saviour and to His mind, knowing Him only in a very distant and superficial way, a knowledge according to the flesh. Unable to free themselves from the notion which the Jews had formed of the Messias and His work, they grasped neither the profound meaning of the work accomplished by the Master, nor the real conditions of His kingdom.

Is it possible to doubt this when one thinks of the questions that the Apostles put to the Saviour at the very moment when He was preparing to leave them in order to rejoin His Father: "Lord, wilt thou at this time restore the kingdom to Israel?" [1]

The uncertainty of a still hesitant love corresponded to the imperfection of their knowledge. Undoubtedly the Apostles were attached to their Master, but still in a very human manner, as was proved by their attitude at the moment of the Passion. When the soldiers came to seize the Saviour, after the scene of the agony, they all abandoned Him, and he among them who had loudly boasted that he would follow Him unto death denied Him three times for fear of sharing His condemnation. Even after the Resurrection, and despite the unimpeachable proofs that He gave of it, Christ found His disciples so little prompt to recognize Him, that he sharply upbraided them for their lack of faith and hardness of heart: *Exprobavit incredulitatem eorum et duritiam cordis*.[2]

Such were the states of mind of the Apostles and the other disciples before Pentecost. Neither the ones nor the others, as we see, were in a suitable state of mind to accomplish the mission which the Saviour had entrusted to them and which had to be completed by the supreme testimony, that of martyrdom. At that time they had neither the courage nor the strength to face the persecutions that the hostility of the Jews and the pagans had in store for the heralds of the Gospel.

But hardly had the Paraclete taken over the minds and the hearts of the disciples when a transformation, no less profound than it was sudden, took place in each one of them. Light broke upon their minds and revealed at last what up to then they had been incapable of understanding. Nothing now escaped them: neither the real meaning of the words and works of the Master, nor the import of His sufferings and humiliations, nor the profound significance of the mystery of the Cross, the mere prospect of which had formerly scandalized and almost revolted them. In all the events of which they had been witnesses they now recognized the fulfillment of the Scriptures. Quite simply it was the realization of what Christ had Himself promised His disciples before leaving them. "But the Advocate (Paraclete), the Holy Spirit, whom the Father will send in my name, he will teach you all

things, and bring to your mind whatever I have said to you."[3]
The Holy Ghost descended upon the disciples gathered at the
Cenacle only to "teach them the whole truth."[4] It is dating from
Pentecost that the disciples know Christ no longer according to
the flesh, but according to the Spirit that lives in each one of them.

At the same time that the Paraclete illumines the intelligence
of the disciples, He enkindles their hearts with an ardent love for
Christ and for the Father who dwells in Him. Because they love
Him now, but with such purity and strength that they have no
other desire save that of bearing witness to their Master before the
world — a witness they will seal with their blood. Filled with
courage and zeal they will soon scatter and go among the pagans,
like sheep among wolves, in order to proclaim the Gospel to them.
St. Peter, who had shown himself to be the weakest among the
Twelve, after having also been the most presumptuous, hastened
to proclaim Christ with an invincible courage. When later they
are manhandled and tortured for the cause of Jesus, the disciples
react with joy: *Ibant gaudentes a conspectu concilii quoniam
digni habiti sunt pro nomine Jesu contumelian pati.*[5]

Such was the admirable transformation which the first Pentecost
saw accomplished in the soul of each one of the disciples gathered
around the Cenacle. Undoubtedly, Christ had already come, He,
the Light of the world, in order to illumine minds and to touch
hearts, but what He could not do from the outside, so to speak,
while He was visible here below, He realized from within and in
an invisible manner by virtue of His Spirit.

By thus transforming each one of the disciples on the day of
Pentecost, the coming of the Paraclete effected at one blow a complete fusion of minds and hearts in the first Christian community.
Gone at last was the time of mean jealousies, petty personal rival-
ries, vain disputes over the question of first place. On the morrow
of Pentecost there was but one heart and soul in the community
of Jerusalem, despite the multitude of believers: *Cor unum et
anima una.*[6] It was, moreover, in the burgeoning Church that the
spirit of Christ, in order to put an end to this baleful dispersion of
peoples of which the episode of Babel remains the symbol, inaugurated the restoration of unity which had been destroyed by the
sin of men.[7]

14

Our Feast of Pentecost

THE RICH AND VERY EXPRESSIVE LITURGY OF Pentecost makes it clearly understood that, on the day we celebrate this mystery, something similar to what took place in the Cenacle of Jerusalem, when the Holy Ghost descended upon the Apostles and disciples of the Lord, takes place in the whole of the Church, albeit without any extraordinary manifestation. In fact, what does the Church petition for all Christians, on this last of the fifty-day paschal period, but that the Holy Ghost, by renewing His presence in souls, illumine them with His brightness, and set them ablaze with the fire of love?

All the living members of the Church have the signal privilege of possessing in themselves this same Holy Ghost of whom the Saviour had the fullness and who so completely transformed the disciples from the very first Pentecost. For by their birth in the divine life they have become, and even in their bodies, the temples of the Holy Spirit.[1] Certain it is that since our baptism, at least if He has not been expelled through our fault, the Holy Ghost, inseparably united to the Father and to the Son from whom He proceeds, lives in us and remains in us according to a mode of presence that itself remains very mysterious.[2] By virtue of this presence, which that Scripture attributes to Him as a personal title, the Holy Ghost dwells not on the surface of the soul, if one can speak thus, like a stranger or a transient guest, but in the deepest and most secret recesses. He dwells in the souls of the just as in His own sanctuary.[3]

However, let us not imagine that this inner presence of the Holy Ghost remains inert and passive. On the contrary it is extremely active. It resembles the presence of fire, for the Spirit lives in souls and dwells therein only in the measure that He acts in them and sanctifies them. He is by this nature, according to the quite characteristic expression of the Greek Fathers, a "living energy." [4]

Here is why it is always opportune to petition God to enlarge His Spirit, even in those who have already received Him. Here is why, in her prayer, the Church never ceases to petition for the sending of the Holy Ghost. But, naturally, she earnestly summons Him, above all and with a particular insistence, on the day in which she makes us liturgically relive the mystery of the Pentecost. For, in order that we may participate in this mystery in an effective and truly fruitful manner, it is not precisely necessary that the Holy Ghost make Himself present where He already resides, but that His activity become even more intense and penetrating in the souls in which He has established Himself, so as always to communicate more largely the riches of divine grace. It is thus that, in the liturgy of Pentecost, the Church petitions the Holy Ghost Himself to fill the hearts of His faithful: *Reple tuorum corda fidelium*,[5] to fill them to their innermost recesses, *Reple cordis intima tuorum fidelium*.[6] The specific fruit of the Eucharistic Sacrifice, celebrated with such magnificence and solemnity on the day of Pentecost, will be, as the Postcommunion of the feast very beautifully tells us, a new and abundant pouring out of the Holy Ghost that will purify our hearts (*Sancti Spiritus corda nostra mundet infusio*), like a sweet and penetrating dew, water the growth of good in them (*et sui roris intima aspersione foecundet*).

On the day of Pentecost, the working of the Holy Ghost in the souls of the faithful will find expression in an abundant effusion of His divine light. Already, the Collect of the Vigil petitions almighty God to let the splendor of His brightness shine on us (*ut claritatis tuae super nos splendor effulgeat*) and to confirm through the illumination of the Holy Ghost (*Sancti Spiriti illustratione confirmet*) the light that those who were born to the life of grace received at baptism.[7] As for the Collect recited on Pentecost itself in the Office as well as in the Mass, it expresses the wish that on this day when the hearts of the faithful were instructed through the light of the Holy Ghost, we may obtain from this same Spirit the true wisdom, that which assures the perfect rectitude of Christian life: *"De nobis in eodem Spiritu recta sapere."*

Since the Holy Ghost, when He descended upon the Apostles, realized the promise of the Saviour by giving them complete illumination on the teaching that they had received from their Master in the course of His mortal life, is it not fitting that on the day of Pentecost, and by virtue of the same promise, the Paraclete illumines us too, and introduces us to the fullness of the truth as the Collect of the Wednesday within the Octave petitions, "May the Holy Comforter, who proceeds from you, O Lord, enlighten our minds and guide us in all truth, as your Son has promised."

This new light that the Holy Ghost spreads in the hearts of His faithful on the day of Pentecost must have the effect of making more clear to them both God's activity in the Church, and the role of Christ Himself, whose glory it is the mission of the Paraclete to make manifest, as this ancient Collect in the Gelasian Sacramentary suggests: "Grant, O Almighty God, that the coming of the Spirit glorify Thy Son by manifesting His majesty to us." [8] In this last solemnity of the paschal mystery, all the souls properly opened to His influence receive from the Holy Ghost the grace to know Christ and His mysteries better; and to know Him with a sharper and more intimate knowledge. Likewise they receive a surer and riper understanding of Holy Scripture and liturgical prayer.

At the first Pentecost, the Paraclete not only illumined the minds of the disciples with His divine light, but, even more, he enkindled their hearts with such a love of the Master, that, transformed into veritable apostles, they immediately became the intrepid witnesses of His Resurrection. Now what the Church desires above all else on the day of Pentecost is that a genuine growth of filial love take place in each one of her living members, under the influence of the Spirit of Christ. Does not the liturgy of Pentecost make us petition, with a downright insistence, for a love of God that is more intense, more sincere and more pure? Each one of the days of the Octave, after the reading of the Epistle and while — through an exceptional departure from liturgical custom [9] — all the officers of the Mass remain humbly kneeling before the

altar, the Church solicits the Holy Ghost to descend into the hearts
of the faithful in order to fill them with Himself and to enkindle
them with the fire of His love.

> *Veni Sancte Spiritus, reple tuorum corda fidelium*
> *Et tui amoris in eis ignem accende.*[10]

Would not one say that in this short but very ardent supplication, the Gregorian melody of which sets off its moving gravity,
the Church concentrates all the force of her prayer? The feast of
Pentecost, in fact, seems to her to be an occasion like no other for
reviving in each one of her members that fire of divine love which
Christ had enkindled in the hearts of His disciples after He had
seated Himself at the right hand of the Father. In one of her
prayers of the Octave, the Church petitions precisely that the Holy
Ghost enkindle us with this same fire that Our Lord Jesus Christ
spread on the earth, in order to kindle there a hearth of loving
warmth.[11] As for the hymn proper to Pentecost, the *Veni Creator*,
sung during the entire Octave twice a day,[12] it petitions that the
Paraclete spread His light in our minds and His love in our hearts:

> *Accende lumen sensibus*
> *Infunde amorem cordibus.*

In the material order no means of purification is more efficacious
than fire. When it is applied to precious metals such as gold or
silver, it strips them of the least dross and frees them from every
alloy. In the order of invisible realities the action of the Holy
Ghost is also sovereignly purifying. In fact when the Holy Ghost
takes hold of a soul nothing can resist His invincible force —
niether the remnants of the former self, nor those yeasty egoisms
that tend to crowd out the full flowering of the baptismal life and
to adulterate the purity of love in our heart. Therefore the liturgy
of Pentecost rightly insists that the Spirit of God, by carrying out
this complete interior renovation which is the pre-eminent fruit of
the paschal solemnities, purify the innermost recesses of our
hearts.[13] Moreover, simply let the Paraclete enter a soul and enkindle it with Charity, and it becomes, by the sole virtue of His
presence, a true temple of glory. Is not this what is suggested by the
petition which the Church makes to God in one of her most beautiful Collects of the Octave:

Praesta, quaesumus, omnipotens et
misericors Deus; ut Spiritus Sanctus
adveniens templum nos gloriae
suae dignanter inhabitando
perficiat.[14]

Earlier we saw that the transformation wrought in each of the disciples by the Holy Ghost at the first Pentecost made itself immediately felt in the whole of the Christian community. There followed spontaneously such a flowering of brotherly love in this nucleus of the nascent Church that all the members seemed to have but one heart and one soul. It was a marvelous unity in praise and thanksgiving. Never had a more intense and fervent prayer been raised towards heaven. Never had apostolic zeal manifested itself with greater vigor and impetus. Never had joy been more profound or more radiant.

Now, it is surely the intention of the Church that every year the recurrence of Pentecost should provoke in the whole of the Mystical Body something akin to what took place formerly in the community at Jerusalem. Is it not above all on such a great day that among Christians moved by the same Spirit, the Spirit of Christ, this perfect concord for which from the start of the fifty-day period the Church asks of God should reach its realization as the precious effect of the paschal solemnities?

"O Lord, fill us with the spirit of your love, so that by receiving this Easter Sacrament our hearts may be united in you." [15] Why should not every feast of Pentecost be marked in the universal Church, as in the individual Churches that constitute her, by a renewal of brotherly love, by a new soaring of the apostolic spirit, by a growth of peace and joy in the unity that Christ restored? Never, undoubtedly, will we see again this extraordinary flowering of charismatic gifts which, in the divine plan, had the aim of making manifest to the eyes of all the first pouring out of the Spirit of Christ. But it remains no less desirable that, having become more conscious of the great supernatural realities that they have been able to relive liturgically in the course of the fifty-day paschal period, all the faithful on this day of Pentecost experience an ardent desire to join in the great prayer of the Church, the liturgical prayer, so as to celebrate with her the *Magnalia Dei.*

15

Pentecost and Confirmation
Note on the Vigil of Pentecost

IN THE 4TH CENTURY THE CUSTOM OF RESERVING more solemn administrations of Baptism for Easter and Pentecost, the two greatest feasts of the fifty-day paschal period, was solidly established in the Roman church. Nothing seems more natural than that Easter Sunday should have become the great baptismal feast of the Christian year, since it is through Baptism and the Eucharist that it is possible for us to participate authentically and in an effective manner in the great mystery of this day, the Resurrection of Christ our Head.[1] As to the choice of Pentecost, this must be attributed to the fact that it ends the fifty-day paschal period of which it is, after Easter to be sure, the most solemn day because of the mystery of which it is the subject. Moreover, the memory of the three thousand persons baptized by St. Peter on the first day of Pentecost [2] probably influenced the choice of this day for the baptismal solemnity, especially since, in the beginning, Confirmation followed immediately the baptism of neophytes.

However that may be, in 398 Pope Siricius, in a letter to Himerius, the bishop of Tarragona, declared the practice of solemnly administering Baptism outside the days of Easter and Pentecost to be contrary to usage.[3] A little later, St. Leo, in turn, censured the Sicilian bishops for not holding to the practice of the Church of Rome by baptizing on the day of Epiphany.[4] According to this same Pope only those persons who, for good cause, had been unable to receive the sacrament on the night of Easter should be admitted to Baptism at Pentecost.

In Rome Baptism was formerly solemnly conferred on the Vigil of Pentecost, as on that of Easter, in the vast Lateran baptistry. Preceded by a vigil of readings and prayers, it was immediately followed by Confirmation, which the pontiff himself administered to the neophytes in an oratory adjoining the baptistry, the oratory of the Cross. It was only after they were baptized and confirmed that the new Christians participated in the sacrifice of the Mass and received for the first time the Body and Blood of Christ. The three rites of initiation thus followed one another in a logical order, one that conforms with the nature of the three sacraments: Baptism, Confirmation and the Eucharist. This is the practice no longer in our days, for Confirmation is usually separated, even considerably so, from Baptism. This latter practice has been, at least for several centuries, the custom in effect in the Latin Church.[5] In fact, the Latin Church, which requires that infants be baptized as soon as possible after birth (*Infantes quamprimum baptizentur*[6]), does not judge it opportune, save for grave cause, that they be confirmed before attaining the age of reason.[7] But, if Confirmation, like Baptism, can be conferred on any day of the year, the Church esteems it sovereignly fitting that the bishop administer this sacrament preferably in the course of the feasts of Pentecost: *Maxime autem decet illud administrari in hebdomoda Pentecostes.*[8]

At the same time, and rightly so, Pentecost presents itself as the liturgical anniversary of our confirmation, and consequently as the day in which it is fitting to renew in ourselves the special virtue of this sacrament and to thank God for it. In fact, of Confirmation it can be said that it is a personal Pentecost for every Christian. Thus, to understand clearly why we receive this sacrament that completes Baptism, and what place it has in our Christian life, we only have to recall what the Holy Ghost accomplished in the souls of those first disciples when He descended upon them with flaming splendor on the day of Pentecost.

After the Resurrection of their Master, Apostles and disciples prudently enclosed themselves in their Cenacle, whose doors St.

John tells us had been closed for fear of the hostility of the Jews. But hardly had the Holy Ghost taken possession of each of them, when we see them quit the Cenacle for the streets in order to bear witness to the risen Christ. Flooded with light, inflamed with love, full of courage and bravery, they no longer feared either insults or torments, but burned, instead, with a desire to bring to the world the message of salvation that Christ had entrusted to them. "For we cannot help speaking of what we have seen and heard," St. Peter resolutely declares before the members of the Sanhedrin.[9] Immediately after Pentecost the Apostles separated in order to announce, first to the Jews and then to the Gentiles, that Christ is dead and risen for the salvation of the world. All must bear witness to Him, even at the price of blood, even to the point of martyrdom.

Now, in a certain measure at least, Confirmation produces in every Christian what the Paraclete realized among the disciples of the Saviour at the time of the first Pentecost. It is, in fact, through the virtue of this sacrament which perfects Baptism that the Christian himself becomes a witness to Christ in the face of the world. According to the Catechism of the Council of Trent "the sacrament of Confirmation strengthens Faith in the hearts of the baptized so that they can confess and glorify Our Lord Jesus Christ." [10] Thus it is correct to say that Confirmation is the sacrament of strength only if we add that this strength is communicated to us with a determined end in view.[11] It is not enough for Christians, through Baptism, to receive the life of the risen Christ for their own sanctification; they must also be rendered capable of making the Faith which they profess radiate on the society surrounding them. For every Christian, by virtue of his Confirmation, is associated, though in a subordinate manner, to the ministry of the Apostles. Undoubtedly, from the moment of Baptism the Holy Ghost penetrates into the soul and sanctifies it, but it is specifically through Confirmation that the Holy Ghost gives the soul the necessary strength to confess and glorify Jesus Christ, even, if necessary, at the price of his blood.

Evidently the simple faithful must bear witness to their Faith, first by the practice of a resolutely Christian life and by becoming, through it, a light in Christ in the midst of a hostile and corrupt world. Is it not precisely this witness that St. Paul demanded from new Christians when he wrote them: "For you were once darkness, but now you are light in the Lord. Walk, then, as children of light. For the fruit of the light is in all goodness and justice and truth"? [12] The Apostle likewise invited the Christians of Phillipi to live like true children of God, without blemish, in the midst of a depraved and perverse generation. "For among these you shine like stars in the world," he told them.[13]

Moreover, if the simple faithful cannot profess their Faith as did the Apostles, through exhortations and speeches, they must at least do so through the expression of praise, by uniting themselves with the Church in order to celebrate the *Magnalia Dei*. As we have already seen, this was precisely the first witness that not only the Apostles bore to God, on the day of Pentecost, but all those who had received the Holy Ghost in the Cenacle.[14] Now the collective witness of a liturgical celebration has a value that increases the more the intervention of the Holy Ghost is more sensible and more manifest in it. Did not St. Paul have in mind a witness of this kind when he wrote to the Ephesians: "Be filled with the Spirit, speaking to one another in psalms and hymns and spiritual songs, singing and making melody in your hearts to the Lord, giving thanks always for all things in the name of our Lord Jesus Christ to God the Father." [15] Do our faithful doubt that taking part with fervor in the liturgical assemblies, and above all in the celebration of the Mass, is to bear the most eloquent and the most decisive of witnesses to God, in front of the world?

It should now be clear how necessary it is for a child to be confirmed as soon as he reaches the age of reason. For it is precisely at that age that he becomes susceptible to bearing witness to the Lord. (Actually, for the child it is already a profession of faith in the face of an unbelieving world to make his First Communion, even if he does not do so as part of a First Communion class.[16]) Need we stress here the very particular importance of Confirmation, most misunderstood of all the Sacraments, in an age like ours where it is a question of bearing witness before a generation very much like that known by St. Paul, and perhaps more fundamentally hostile to Christ and to the Church?

All Christians, therefore, should be eager to celebrate the feast of Pentecost as the anniversary of their own Confirmation. Pentecost, as the liturgy of this great solemnity superabundantly proves, is indeed the day which, each year, authentically renews the mystery of the Holy Ghost coming here below to fill the living members of the Church with His divine light, to enkindle them with the fire of love, and to clothe them with an ever more powerful strength in view of the witness that they must bear to the risen Christ before the world.

16

The Joy of Pentecost

W<small>HEN, ON THE EVENING OF EASTER, THE LORD</small> manifested Himself to His Apostles for the first time, the latter, according to St. John, experienced a feeling of joy at the sight of their arisen Master: *Gavisi sunt discipuli viso Domino.* This joy could only grow warmer and keener during the forty days that preceded the departure of Christ, at the end of a series of different apparitions which finally convinced the Apostles and disciples beyond all doubt of the reality of His Resurrection. The return of Christ to heaven, far from causing His disciples the least sadness, was for them, as we have already said, a new motive for joy, since, according to St. Luke, they returned to Jerusalem *cum gaudio magno.* But it is difficult for us to imagine what the happiness of the Apostles and disciples was when, on the day of Pentecost, there descended upon each one of them the One whom they were awaiting as the object of their most ardent desire, the Paraclete. This overwhelming joy that followed the pouring out of the Holy Ghost took such forms that the crowd attributed these disciples' conduct to drinking. In fact, the excitement of the disciples leaving the Cenacle to celebrate the *Magnalia Dei* with such enthusiasm was certainly drunkenness, but that spiritual drunkenness which St. Ambrose sings of in one of his hymns.[1] Since the joy with which the disciples were filled flowed from the Holy Ghost, nothing could temper its radiance. It was a continual, abiding joy. It shines out in the first Christian community as this is described for us in the Acts of the Apostles. It was evidently the Spirit of Pentecost that animated these brotherly love feasts where, St. Luke tells us, the Christians took their food in gladness and simplicity of heart, *cum exultatione et simplicitate cordis*.[2] "The life of the primitive Church," writes Dom Vonier, "was a transport of joy in the Holy Ghost." [3] Nor did the Spirit of Christ lack means — the Holy Eucharist — to keep alive and to increase in souls this Pentecostal joy.

After having received the Paraclete, the Apostles experienced the great joy of preaching Christ and of bearing witness to Him, while undergoing multiple ordeals for the glory of His name. We have already given prominence to the very meaningful text of the book of the Acts which shows them leaving the Sanhedrin full of joy (*gaudentes*) because they had been judged worthy of suffering for the name of Jesus.[4] Later, St. Paul, when he had been filled with the Holy Ghost as the result of his conversion, also experienced — amidst the sufferings and tribulations his apostolic zeal had earned for him — the incomparable joy of proclaiming Christ and of spreading the message of salvation in souls. This deep joy of St. Paul is expressed above all in his Epistles written in captivity, when he already glimpsed the martyrdom that was to crown his career. "But even if I am made the libation for the sacrifice and service of your Faith, I joy and rejoice with you," he writes the Philippians. [5] How many were the martyrs, during the beginnings of the Church, who gave themselves up to torture intoxicated, like Ignatius of Antioch, with a divine joy, the joy of Pentecost.

It was, moreover, on the same day in which the Spirit of Christ spread in her and filled her with power that the Church inaugurated her first conquests. These are celebrated with as much vigor as lyricism in the pre-eminent Psalm of Pentecost, the Psalm *Exsurgat Deus*, a true canticle of appreciation and gladness which in its final part makes us glimpse the supreme and universal triumph of the Redeemer.[6]

If the feast of Ascension, which has caused us to relive the mystery of the Saviour ascending to heaven, and to renew in our hearts the hope of joining Him there, has filled with joy all the members of the Body of which Christ is the Head, what must not be our joy when we celebrate Pentecost? For on this very holy day, every year in the whole Church there is a new, large and abundant pouring out of the One who, at the end of the fifty-day paschal period, returns to illuminate us with His divine light and enkindle us with the fire of His love! Is it not fitting that each feast of Pentecost, by making us further feel the interior assistance of the Paraclete, also increases the joy flowing therefrom? This joy the Church petitions precisely as the fruit of the solemnity, *"Da nobis in eodem Spiritu recta sapero; et de ejus semper consolatione gaudere."* [7] Moreover, since joy is one of the fruits of the Holy Ghost, according to St. Paul, it seems completely natural that, by becoming more and more intense, the action of the Holy Ghost in our souls is expressed by a continual growth of this Christian joy. Baptism has deposited the seeds of this joy in our hearts, and those seeds develop from year to year, during the paschal feasts, until they reach full flower in the joy of heaven. Finally, Pentecost being the day on which the paschal work possesses all its perfection, it is truly right and just, as the Preface sings, that the whole world is jubilant with unrestrained joy: *Quapropter profusis gaudiis, totus in orbe terrarum mundus exsultat.*

17

The Week of Pentecost

Begun on easter sunday, the joyous fifty-day period should normally end on Pentecost itself, which was formerly called *Pascha clausam*, "Easter closed." But for many centuries now the paschal time is prolonged during the entire week that follows Pentecost and does not "expire," according to the expression of the rubrics, until Ember Saturday, immediately after the celebration of the Mass: *Post missam expirat tempus paschale.* This prolongation of the paschal time is due to the institution of the thoroughly warranted Octave of Pentecost.[1] The feast of Easter having itself been prolonged for a week, the week *in Albis*, in order to permit the neophytes of the paschal night to become more aware of the riches of their Baptism and to give thanks to God, it was inevitable that Pentecost, the second baptismal solemnity of the Christian year, would also be provided with an Octave possessing the same privileges as that of Easter.

Let us immediately say that there is no serious reason either to regret the existence of this Octave, or to desire its suppression.[2] It is true that certain writers point out that if it is prolonged for a whole week the paschal time will no longer numerically represent the ancient fifty-day period, since it numbers fifty-six days instead of fifty, the traditional figure whose mysterious symbolism the Church Fathers, basing themselves on Scripture, were pleased to stress. But this objection is hardly of any importance, because in the eyes of the Church the days of the Octave morally are but one with the day of the feast itself. Consequently, the number fifty preserves all the exactness, liturgically.[3]

Some also find it very regrettable that the Octave of Pentecost, every year, inevitably coincides with a week of Ember Days.[4] As the result of this unfortunate coincidence, the supplementary paschal week, some assert, is provided with a hybrid liturgy in which the expression of joy contrasts strangely with that of penitence. Does not the fast of Embers Days seem incompatible with the gladness that characterizes the fifty-day paschal period?

How answer this question? It will not take us long to see that, despite the foregoing assertion, the liturgy of the Octave is quite far from having the hybrid character attributed to it. We shall see that the texts that relate to Pentecost offer no real discordance with those that come from the Ember Days.[5] We do not claim along with certain liturgists of the Middle Ages, whose ingeniousness was too often excessive, that the fast of Ember Days is a "fast of joy" a "fast that one might call ecstatic" and that "the delights of the Spirit throw the soul into a state of intoxication that makes her forget the fast."[6] Though we disregard this mystical explication, which today makes us smile, it no less remains true that the liturgy of Ember Days despite its penitential character — which is undeniable — in no way excludes the expression of joy. Proof of this is furnished by the September Ember Days: for most of the elements of which the September Ember Wednesday Mass is composed breathe a vivid gladness, from the Introit *Exsultate Deo* to the antiphon of the Communion, which ends on these words: *Gaudium etenim Domini est fortitudo nostra*. "The joy of the Lord is our strength."[7] Moreover, the observance of the Ember Days is not exclusively a remedy for our weakness, or a means of periodically making reparation for the sins that derive from human frailty, since St. Leo himself, who has formulated — and in a most authentic way — the thinking of the Church on this subject, presents us the fast of the month of December as a fast of thanksgiving for the completion of the harvest: *pro consumata perceptione omnium fructuum terrae*.[8] Can one, therefore, claim that the fast is irreconcilable with the paschal liturgy, which is a liturgy of thanksgiving?

Instead of wishing for its disappearance, let us rather accept this Octave of Pentecost, such as it is today and has been for many centuries, with its liturgy so complexly rich in light and life.[9]

The Octave of Pentecost, like that of Easter, involves the cele-

bration of a stational Mass for each day of the week. It is completely natural for the station of Wednesday to be the Church of
Santa Maria Maggiore, that of Friday the Church of the Holy
Apostles, and that of Saturday the Church of St. Peter, since it was
always the custom in Rome to celebrate the stational Masses of
Ember Days in each one of these three sanctuaries. Given the role
that St. Peter played in the first Pentecost, no place could seem
more fitting than the Vatican basilica for celebrating the mystery
of the Holy Ghost descending upon the Apostles and vivifying the
Church on the very day on which the mystery is commemorated.
The same reason probably led to the choice of another church,
dedicated to the head of the Apostles, as the stational place for
Monday: the Church of St. Peter in Chains. The stational Mass
of Tuesday of Pentecost is no longer celebrated in the Church of
St. Paul, as on Easter Tuesday, but in the Church of St. Anastasia,
today a rather modest sanctuary, but formerly, as a basilica of
the imperial court, in the first rank of Roman titular churches.[10]
As for the Mass of Thursday, which is certainly of a later origin
than the others, it is sung at the Church of St. Lawrence Outside
the Walls, on the tomb of the illustrious deacon whom the Romans,
quite properly, considered as the third protector of the city.

When Pope Gregory VII definitively fixed the date of the Summer Ember Days, there were still two distinct formularies, that of
the week of Pentecost, and that of the Ember Days. Soon these
two formularies were merged into one, the one we have today.
Now, although they derive from two very different sources, the
liturgical texts of the Octave were so aptly chosen and blended
that no shocking discordance is perceived between them. It was
thus that the readings which are given on the Saturday Ember
Days were visibly chosen with a concern to link them to Pentecost,
which among the Jews was the Feast of the Spring Harvest.[11] The
first reading is none other than the passage from Joel which contains the promise of this wondrous pouring out of the Holy
Ghost, whose realization St. Peter was to confirm on the same day
of Pentecost.[12] Taken from Leviticus, the second reading summarizes the prescriptions relative to the manner of celebrating
the feast of Shabuoth, that is to say, the Jewish Pentecost, "this
day most celebrated and most holy," *dies celeberrimus atque sanc-*

tissimus, which, along with the exclusion of all servile work, included the offering of a new sacrifice.[13] The third reading, taken from Deuteronomy, recalls the obligation that Moses himself imposed on the Israelites to offer the first of all the fruits of their earth to God, in order to thank Him for having delivered them from bondage in Egypt and led them to a land flowing with milk and honey.[14] Does not this passage especially fit these new Christians, who on the same night of Pentecost are wrested from Satan's empire, through Baptism and Confirmation, only to be introduced into the kingdom of Christ? In the fourth reading it is the Lord Himself who promises Moses to reward the faithfulness of his people with abundant harvests.[15] Already the passage from Joel, which is sung instead of an Epistle at the Mass of Friday, exhorts Israel to rejoice and to offer thanks because of the wonders God has done for her.[16] Evidently, in the thought of the Church, the abundance of earthly goods, on which these readings dwell, is the figure and image of spiritual riches which, since Pentecost, the Paraclete had poured in profusion on the new people of God, the Christian people.

The small alleluiatic versicles that follow each of the readings of the Old Testament very beautifully give prominence to the activity of the Holy Ghost,[17] and the discreet allusions to the fast contained in several Collects of the pre-Mass do not impair the paschal tonality of the Saturday of Pentecost.

The Octave of Pentecost, whose liturgy is so rich in its complexity, has the great advantage of making us relive, as largely and deeply as possible, this mystery of the pouring out of the Holy Ghost, the capital importance of which in the supernatural economy cannot be exaggerated. Whereas the paschal octave presents Baptism above all as the authentic means of participating in the Resurrection of Christ, the week of Pentecost incites Christians to recall that, through Baptism followed by Confirmation, they have become living temples of the Holy Ghost. It is precisely this that the antiphon of the Introit of Ember Saturday sets off in relief:

"The charity of God is poured forth in our hearts, alleluia! by his Spirit, dwelling within us, alleluia, alleluia!" [18]

Already, as we have seen previously, the Church in a Collect of the Wednesday of Pentecost petitions God to grant that the

Holy Ghost, by coming to dwell in our hearts, may make of us a temple of His glory: *"Ut Spiritus Sanctus adveniens, templum nos gloriae suae dignanter inhabitando perficiat."* [19]

The Epistles of the first days of the Octave throw a vivid light on the activity of the Holy Ghost in the new-born Church. We hear St. Peter, in the presence of the Jews, bear witness, on the day of Pentecost, of the realization of the divine promises; [20] we see the grace of the Holy Ghost spread in Samaria and as far as the pagan nations; [21] we witness the prodigies of all kinds that are accomplished by the Apostles under the impulse of the Paraclete.[22] These different readings give great prominence to the vivifying role exercised by the One who, since Pentecost, has become the soul of the Church.

For their part, the Gospels of this same week remind Christians, more or less recently baptized and confirmed, of the primordial importance of Faith and of docility towards the true Shepherd,[23] as well as of the necessity of maintaining and developing this supernatural life — of which the Holy Ghost is the beginning — through the Eucharist.[24]

Thanks to the existence of the Octave, the ordination of priests and other clerics on Ember Saturday takes place during the celebration of the mystery of Pentecost. Therein lies an advantage the interest of which it would be impossible not to recognize. For there is no more favorable day in the year, perhaps, for asking God to pour the sanctifying Spirit over the persons whom the Church herself destines to continue the work of the Apostles and who, themselves, must directly co-operate in the building-up of the Body of Christ, through the sanctity of their example and the exercise of their ministry.

It seems to us that the week of Pentecost usefully serves as a transition between the closing of the paschal solemnities and these last months of the liturgical year in which the Church, after having renewed and fortified herself through the celebration of the redemptive mystery, resumes the ordinary course of her pilgrimage towards the celestial Jerusalem, while waiting for the Bridegroom, whose return she ardently desires, coming to meet her, radiant in all His glory.

PART THREE

The Spirit of Pentecost and the
Life of the Church

18

After Pentecost: The Sunday Liturgy

As the culminating point of the work of Christ and the conclusion of the paschal mystery, Pentecost was the supreme object of the long preparation carried on during the entire course of the Old Testament until the coming of the Saviour into this world. For it was the Messias, promised and awaited since the original Fall, whose task it would be to establish a new order and to inaugurate the kingdom of God over all the peoples of the earth, through an abundant pouring out of the Holy Ghost, whose fullness He would possess in Himself. It is certain that the Old Testament was oriented in a progressive manner towards the pouring out through Christ of the immanent gift of the sanctifying Spirit. The blessing that God had promised Abraham was not totally realized, according to St. Paul, and did not extend to the pagans except on the day when the latter received the Spirit coming from Christ.[1]

Moreover, everything that the Saviour Himself accomplished here below, from His Incarnation up to the Sacrifice of the Cross, or rather up to His glorious Ascension, was ordained for the accomplishment of the divine promise — for the pouring out of the new Spirit. In realizing this promise, the Holy Ghost, who is the Spirit of Truth, the *Spiritus veritatis*,[2] bore witness to the fidelity of God.

But after having been the object of divine preparations, Pentecost became the point of departure for a new era. Dating from Pentecost, the ancient law promulgated on Mt. Sinai gave place to the Gospel.[3]

With Pentecost there actually began — in the form of Christ's

77

Church here below — that universal kingdom of God which is destined to find its full realization in the glory of eternity. If it is true that the Holy Ghost is the soul of the Church, it can very well be said that the Church was born on the day of Pentecost. "From whatever angle one envisages the work of Pentecost," writes Dom Vonier, "the best definition that one can give it is that through it was born the Church. Undoubtedly Christ had already revealed the Faith, established the hierarchy, instituted the sacraments; the principles of supernatural life had been confirmed through Him, because He did not come to abolish but to fulfill. The Church, however, had not been born. . . . To assert that the Church was born at Pentecost is simply to say that at that moment a new life came into being: total Christian life with its renewal of sanctity." [4]

It is precisely the mystery of Pentecost that the long liturgical period which begins on Trinity Sunday and ends at the beginning of Advent makes us re-live. By virtue of their Baptism all Christians participate in this mystery, which is continued and developed in the Church through the centuries.

Now, after having, since Christmas, relived liturgically the different mysteries of Christ with the Church; after having renewed and fortified our Christian life through the celebration of the paschal solemnities, we still, during the weeks that separate Pentecost from Advent, must follow the Church in the pilgrimage that under guidance of the Paraclete she carries on here below, hastening towards the celestial city in expectation of the great day of the Lord when, yielding at last to the appeals of His Bride, Christ will lead her into glory.

We have no intention here of lingering, even briefly, over the structure of these Sundays after Pentecost, whose liturgical composition — as the result of many circumstances — is far from having the coherence and the unity presented by the Sundays of Lent, for example, or of the paschal time. We shall content ourselves with noting some characteristic features of these Sundays after Pentecost where the liturgy gives prominence to diverse aspects of the permanent activity of the Paraclete in the life of the Church. For, on Pentecost, the Spirit of Christ descended here below in order to remain until the end of time, as the Saviour Himself foretold to His apostles: "And I will ask the Father and he will give you another Advocate to dwell with you forever (*ut maneat vobiscum in aeternum*)." [5] The work of Pentecost, therefore, is not finished. It continues in the Church of which the Holy Ghost remains the vivifying principle. It is the Holy Ghost, as a Collect of the Missal says, who sanctifies and governs the body of the Church in the totality of her members: *cujus Spiritu, totum corpus Ecclesiae sanctificatur et regitur.*[6]

Ever since the Holy Ghost took up his dwelling in her, the Church here below has never known and will never know the repose and the felicity which the elect enjoy in heaven. She is, if one may use the expression, the Church ambulatory and militant, ever on the march towards the object of her hope. All Christians share the duty of uniting themselves with the Church in this fast march, because it is the objective of all to arrive, without delay and without sin, at the end of the pilgrimage. This is the preoccupation that comes to light in many of the liturgical texts of the time after Pentecost in which the Church, in order to encourage and excite us, recalls the divine promises. In one Collect, she has us petition God for that fervent Charity which obtains the realization of His promises that surpass all desire: "*Ut te in omnibus et super omnia diligentes, promissiones tuas, quae omne desiderium superant consequamur.*" [7] In another Collect, the Church shows us that in order to merit what the Lord has promised us, it is first necessary to obtain the grace to love all the commandments He Himself has given us: "*Ut mereamur quod promittis fac nos amare quod praecipis.*" [8] Elsewhere, we ask God to shower His mercy upon us so that by running towards His promises we may be deserving of sharing in the heavenly rewards: *Ut ad tua promissa currentes, coelestium bonorum facias esse consortes.*[9] Of course, the Church counts on the support of the Lord so that we may run without hindrance towards the object of His divine promises: "*Ut ad promissiones tuas sine offensione, curramus.*" [10] For we must always take care, as the Epistle of the ninth Sunday warns us, not to imitate the Jews who for having succumbed to sinful desires and turned to grumbling were laid low in the desert, so that only a small number reached the Prom-

ised Land.[11] The object of these promises towards which the
Church strives to take us along is, of course, our complete participation in the glory of the risen Christ, the completion of our
Redemption. Now upon whom does the mission of leading us to
the object of the promises devolve if not upon the Holy Ghost?
Undoubtedly the promises have already been realized in principle
in Christ Himself. It is in Him, our Head, that God has raised up
our nature and placed it at His right hand in the heavens.[12] But
the Holy Ghost was sent down, on the day of Pentecost, precisely
for the purpose of extending to all the members of the Church
what had already been accomplished in the person of her Head.
The Holy Ghost was given to us as the earnest of our future glorification.[13] It is, St. Paul tells us, a pledge, a title, to the possession
of God, this heritage that must be the fruit of our redemption.[14]
For the Holy Ghost makes us heirs of God and joint heirs of
Christ: *heredes Dei, et coheredes Christi.*[15]

For as long a time as the promises will not have been completely
realized, for as long a time as her members will not have been
glorified in their very flesh, the Church will continue to live in
the realm of Hope. That is why the virtue of Hope occupies so
great a place in the liturgy of the time after Pentecost. The Mass
of the first Sunday, which unfortunately is almost never sung,[16]
opens indeed with an Introit in which the Church resolutely af-
firms her Hope and the joy that flows therefrom: "O Lord, I have
hoped for your mercy; my heart has rejoiced in your salvation. I
will sing to the Lord, who has given me all good." [17] In the
Collect of this Sunday, the Church addresses herself to God as
being the strength of all who place their Hope in Him: *Deus in
te sperantium fortitudo.* Another time she invokes Him as the
Protector of those who hope in His mercy: *Protector in te sperantium Deus.*[18]

The different chants of which these Sunday Masses are composed — antiphons, versicles and responses — ceaselessly give prominence to the place due to Hope in Christian life. Sometimes the
Church exhorts us to the beneficial practice of this virtue: "Let
those hope in you who cherish your name, O Lord." [19]

"Blessed is the man who hopes in him." [20] "It is better to have confidence in the Lord than to rely on princes." [21] Sometimes, and even more frequently, she places on our lips the expression of absolute confidence in God, "I have hoped in you, let me never be put to shame." *In te Domine speravi, non confundar in aeternum.*[22] This verse of the 30th Psalm and others similar to it recur with a particular frequency in our Sunday liturgy.[23]

There is no Mass, so to speak, where one does not find, in one form or another, the affirmation of our Hope in the mercy of God and in His fidelity.

The time which follows Pentecost, more than any other, is the time for our Hope to be affirmed. For Christian Hope is not like earthly hope, ever uncertainly resting upon fragile probabilities or vain illusions. Supported by the Holy Ghost, whom God Himself gave to us in order to realize His promises, Christian Hope, in contrast, rests on an absolute certainty. By His presence alone in the soul, He whom we call "the gift of God," *Donum Dei altissimi,* is the pledge and the solid foundation of our Hope. The Paraclete enters into us only in order to act, to vivify us, sanctify us, and to transform us into the image of Christ, at least if we oppose no sinful resistance to His activity. It is likewise through the Paraclete that our mortal bodies will also be glorified. "But if the Spirit of him who raised Jesus from the dead dwells in you, then he who raised Jesus Christ from the dead will also bring to life your mortal bodies because of his Spirit who dwells in you," *vivificabit et mortalia corpora vestra, propter inhabitantem Spiritum in vobis.*[24]

We are not unaware that, if left to our own forces, we are absolutely incapable of arriving at the goal of our pilgrimage, our glorification in Christ. The Church, in her Collects of the Sundays after Pentecost, does well to make us recognize our impotence and the necessity for the help of grace which must predispose us and follow us in the least details of our activity.[25] Without the Lord, human weakness can achieve nothing: *Sine te nihil potest mortalis infirmitas;*[26] without Him, we can do nothing to please Him, *tibi sine te placere non possumus;*[27] without Him, nothing is strong, nothing is holy, *Sine quo nihil est validum, nihil sanctum.*[28] These, and many similar humble confessions of our impotence echo the words that the Saviour Himself addressed to His

own disciples, *Sine me nihil potestis facere*: "For without me
you can do nothing." [29] But is is precisely from the Paraclete, who
since Pentecost dwells in the Church and animates each one of
her members, that we receive all the spiritual riches, the grace, the
virtues and gifts that are ordained for the entire realization of the
divine promises, for our glorification. It is likewise the Holy Ghost
who inspires the prayer of the Church, and who makes us petition
for the coming of the kingdom of God. For the Holy Ghost is the
"Paraclete" in the sense peculiar to the word, that is to say it is He
who assists the Church and guides her, while she journeys here
below, until her rendezvous with the Lord: *donec veniat*.

The march of the Hebrews towards the Promised Land is the
prophetic figure of the pilgrimage towards heaven which the new
people of God accomplish here below. On their route the Christian people also encounter continual obstacles to be surmounted,
numerous shoals to be avoided, enemies of all kinds to be fought,
and ordeals to be endured without complaining so as to arrive at
the end of the journey. It is for God to make Himself the ruler and
the guide of His people, as this Collect of the Third Sunday, which
perfectly summarizes the post-Pentecost liturgy, petitions:

"O God, you are the protector of all those who trust in you,
and without You nothing is strong, nothing is holy. Be ever more
merciful towards us, and rule and guide us (*te rectore, te duce*)
that we may use the good things of this life in such a way as not
to lose the blessings of eternal life."

Now God sent the Paraclete precisely for the purpose of being
our guide here below, and of introducing us to the entire truth. [30]
The Holy Ghost has the mission to illumine our steps, to invest
us with His strength, to protect us against everything that can
harm us. Is this not what the Church asks of the Holy Ghost on
the very day of Pentecost:

> Far from us drive our hellish foe,
> True peace unto us bring,
> And through all perils lead us safe
> Beneath thy sacred wing. [31]

The Spirit of Pentecost and the Witness of the Holiness Note on the Devotion of Saints

BEFORE LEAVING THE WORLD AND ASCENDING TO heaven, the Saviour had promised His disciples that he would send them the Spirit of Truth, and that this Spirit would glorify Him, just as He Himself had glorified the Father: *Ille me clarificabat, quia* de meo accipiet et *annuntiabit vobis*.[1] Now, since Pentecost, the glorification of Christ is continued here below with no discontinuity, through the sanctification of the members of His Mystical Body, which is particularly the work of the Holy Ghost. It is above all because He sanctifies souls that the Holy Ghost can be called the "glorifier" of Christ.[2] The Holy Ghost glorifies Christ by communicating the holiness of their Head to the members of the Body. Is it not, in fact, the never-failing holiness of the Church which is the principal witness to the holiness of the Saviour, and therefore also to His divinity? Only Christ is substantially holy, and we proclaim Him such, *Tu solus sanctus,* because He is the Son of God and because God alone is holy. Among us other creatures there is holiness only in the measure in which, thanks to the Spirit which dwells and acts in us since Baptism, we participate in the divine life of Jesus Christ and identify ourselves with Him. Has not St. Paul declared that "before the foundation of the world God chose us in Christ, to the end that we should be holy and without blemish in his sight"?[3] To be holy is to be in conformity with Christ, not simply by virtue of an exterior resemblance, in the manner of a copy that reproduces a beautiful model, but by virtue of a vital assimilation. In order to be holy, according to the beautiful expression of the Apostle, we must "clothe" ourselves internally with Jesus Christ. He in whom the holiness of Christ continues, flowers and shines forth is truly holy and can say in all strictness what St. Paul said of himself. "It is no longer I that live, but Christ lives in me." [4]

Thus the glorification of Christ consists essentially in the fact that, since Pentecost, the holiness of the Head continuously spreads itself in the members of His Mystical Body in order to shine forth here below and shed its rays on the world. Is it not a wondrous and truly divine thing that, since the beginning of the Church and by the hidden power of the vivifying Spirit dwelling in her, the holiness of Christ, in all its many aspects, could manifest itself everywhere and always in so marvelously many forms?

Since the day of Pentecost, immediately after the descent of the Paraclete, how far has that little first Christian community — embracing the holiest of all the creatures of heaven and earth, the Virgin Mary, surrounded by the Apostles of the Saviour and by His first disciples — cast its ray! Hardly did the Church begin to conquer the world when her growing vitality brought upon her the most frightful persecutions on the part of pagan society. But these were prolonged for more than three centuries only for the purpose of having the holiness of the martyrs burst forth in its full brilliance. When she enjoyed peace, the Church everywhere, in the cities and deserts, saw the holiness of ascetics, of confessors and virgins, spread and flower in her bosom. It was then, with the Anthonys, the Pachomiuses, and all those who walked in their footsteps, that the magnificent flowering of monastic holiness came into being. And then came the Middle Ages, in which robust Faith could find its full expression only in that innumerable multitude of Saints of all condition, popes, kings, bishops, monks, clerics and lay people, nobles and serfs who sprang up in every place where the Gospel had been planted.

No, the holiness of Christ has never ceased since Pentecost, and it will never cease to flower upon the earth until the end of time, not even in the darkest and most agonizing periods of the history of the Church like the one we are traversing right now. On the contrary, when Faith seems to slacken and Charity to grow cold, the Spirit of God raises up, in both sexes and in great number, those ardent imitators of Christ who, more by the light of their personal holiness than through external activity, help build up Christian life anew. For the Church counts not only upon the Saints whose memory she honors on November 1, the elect who had the privilege of being raised to her altars or whose names figure in the martyrologies, but also upon that throng of faithful souls who, under the influence of the Holy Ghost, have quietly and unobtrusively spread the beautiful fragrance of Jesus Christ.

This permanent manifestation of the holiness of the Saviour on earth, for which we are obligated to the active presence of His Spirit, is all the more glorious for the One who is its beginning and its Divine Model because it presents a democratic character: holiness is not the privilege of a chosen portion of humanity. The Saints, those in whom the ransoming Blood of Christ manifests its power, have come from all nations and races; they are of all ages and of both sexes, of all tongues and social conditions, and it is therefore that we sing in the Antiphon of the Feast of All Saints: "You have ransomed us in Your blood, Lord our God, from all nations and tribes and peoples and tongues." [5]

Since grace does not destroy nature but perfects it, each one of these elect loses nothing of his personal physiognomy, nor the characteristics peculiar to him, in reproducing Christ. Thus it is strictly true to say that, in the case of every Saint, there is no one else just like him or her in his particular way of putting into practice the precepts of God's Law: *Non est inventus similis illi qui conservaret legem Excelsi.*[6] Neither can two members be found in the Mystical Body who reflect the holiness of the Head to the same degree: *"Stella a stella differt in claritate,"* as St. Paul tells us.[7] The glory of the elect is all the more effulgent the more the action of the Holy Ghost is exercised in them with greater vigor and makes them further resemble their divine pattern, Christ Jesus. Naturally, it is to the Mother of God, the chosen sanctuary of the Holy Ghost, *Sacrarium Spiritus Sancti,* and veritable mirror of the Sun of justice, that God has accorded the honor of reflecting the holiness of her own Son with the greatest perfection.

However, this multitude of elect of every condition, of every national or racial descent, and of both sexes, whom the Church celebrates on All Saints' Day and who under their different aspects represent the pre-eminent holiness of Christ, does not constitute a confused mass, nor an assemblage of more or less disparate elements. The Spirit of God, by filling the Saints with the riches of grace, made them resemble their sovereign Model only in order to establish among them, in an admirable diversity, that mysterious oneness which before dying the Saviour Himself petitioned from His Father as the supreme fruit of His sacrifice: *Ut sint unum sicut et nos unum sumus.*[8]

During long centuries the veneration of the Saints occupied only a very limited place in the first part of the liturgical year. The feasts of Saints included in the old Roman sacramentaries are few in number between the beginning of Advent and Pentecost. It is only after this latter solemnity that the feasts of the Saints are more numerous and more important. This disposition was very logical. For it was necessary that nothing should interrupt the sequence of the mysteries of the Lord which follow one another from Advent until Pentecost, and that nothing should hinder the faithful from uniting themselves attentively to the celebration of these mysteries. For this reason the Roman Church did not consent until very late to the inclusion of some rare feasts of Saints in the Lenten season.[9] But after Pentecost nothing could seem more fitting than to honor the memory of those blessed whom the Holy Ghost, through His virtue, transformed into the image of Christ so as to glorify Christ in them. For it is indeed Christ Himself, the glorious Christ, whom we see reappear not only in the Sunday liturgy but also in the feasts of the Saints which, from Pentecost onwards, follow one another uninterruptedly until Advent.[10]

Yes, it is Christ, source and model of all holiness, whom the Church celebrates each time that she celebrates this or that of these glorious elect who, on the calendar, occupy the last part of the Christian year. "God manifests Himself in His saints," *Gloriosus Deus in sanctis suis,"* we sing in a Mass in honor of the martyrs.[11] Is not feting the saints above all a bearing of witness to the victory of Christ according as, since Pentecost, and through the fecundity of His Spirit, that victory is prolonged and comes to flower in these many elect who, after having in one way or another participated in the Passion of the Saviour, now reign with Him in the glory of heaven?

Naturally the action of the Paraclete reveals His power and His fecundity above all among the Saints who were most intimately united with Christ in the work of our Redemption. This is why the Church most rightly deems that the Apostles have the right to greater honors from us than do the other Saints.[12] Were they not chosen,[13] called and trained by Jesus Himself in order to become His most intimate collaborators, his "friends"?[14] Is it not to the Apostles that we owe our knowledge of Christ, whose activities, miracles and words they have more or less directly transmitted to us, either in the Gospels or in the Epistles? But, moreover, they reproduced in themselves, in their own lives, and under different aspects, the holiness of their Master. They lived in the same conditions as He did, they followed Him in His humbleness, His obedience and His poverty. Like Him, they worked with their hands and preached the Gospel of the Kingdom; like Him they worked miracles; they drove out devils, healed the sick, and raised up the dead; like Him they were the butt of persecutions, they knew failures. They drank from His chalice: *Calicem domini biberunt et amici Dei sunt*.[15] They too sowed the Church in their blood: *plantaverunt Ecclesiam in sanguine suo*.[16] But they actually became Apostles of Christ, His perfect representatives, only on the day of Pentecost, when the Holy Ghost assumed control of them in order to make them fully like their Master and Model, and to enlighten and sustain them in the accomplishment of their mission. It is to the Spirit of Pentecost that the Apostles owe their marvelous transformation in Christ.

In truth, what we celebrate in these different feasts of the Apostles, spread throughout the liturgical year, is Christ Himself as He relives here below in the person of His most immediate and most faithful collaborators. Therefore it is completely natural that the Apostles should now enjoy a privileged devotion in the Church, and that the feast of the Apostles Peter and Paul, always so close to Pentecost, should have become one of our most glorious

liturgical solemnities. Not all the Apostles, it is true, are equally
known to us. And about several of them we know but little —
legend, in their case, having too often substituted for history. But
what does it matter? In the thought of the Church, the Apostles
are inseparably united through the same Spirit, the Spirit of Pentecost, and the homage that we render to each one of them ex-
tends as far and as high as the person of their Head — Christ,
King of the Apostles.

After the Apostles, the first place in our veneration belongs
to the "triumphant cohort of martyrs," [17] an ever more numerous
cohort whom the Church cherishes with a veritable tenderness
and whom she surrounds with her visible predilection.[18] Nothing
could be more natural, since the martyrs assume the glorious privilege of representing the Saviour through the centuries in His
immolation and in His triumph. But like the most illustrious
among them, St. Stephen, all owe their heroic courage in the
midst of torments, and the wisdom of the answers they gave their
persecutors, to the assistance of the Holy Ghost. It is rightly reported in regard to St. Stephen that his adversaries could not
withstand the wisdom and the Saint who spoke: *Non poterant
resistere sapientiae, et Spiritui qui loquebatur.*[19] Moreover, Christ
had announced to His disciples that they would be delivered up
to judgment, but that the Holy Ghost would take it upon Himself to confound their accusers: *Non enim vos estis qui loquamini
sed Spiritus Patris vestri qui loquitur in vobis.*[20] Thanks to the
Spirit of whom he had the fullness, St. Stephen, at the very moment of his agony, could glimpse "the glory of God, and Jesus
standing at the right hand of of God." [21] Is there a martyr whose
death more resembles that of Christ than the death of St. Stephen
did?

How many liturgical prayers exalt the martyrs imitating Christ
in His passion by their sufferings! "Heroes of holiness," sings one
response, "they have spilt their blood for the Lord, they loved
Christ during their lives, they imitated Him in their deaths, and
because of that they have merited the crown of the triumphant." [22]
There is no doubt that the office of martyrs, like that of the
Apostles, principally celebrates Christ Himself, whom the Church
invokes as "the glorious King of martyrs." In the martyrs there is

a hymn addressed to Christ, "Thou art the victor; *Tu vincis in martyribus.*" [23]

Since the martyrs represent Christ in the mystery of His immolation and His triumph, it is entirely natural that Psalms or verses of Psalms are placed on our lips, which directly apply either to the passion of the Saviour, or to His exaltation. Such is, for example, the case of this antiphon that serves as the Introit to the Mass of a martyr during the paschal time: *Protexisti me Deus, a conventu malignantium, alleluia: a multitudine operantium iniquitatem, alleluia.*[24] In commenting on the 63rd Psalm from which this verse was taken, St. Augustine points out that if many of the martyrs had experienced what the Psalmist had prophesied, it is with the Head of the martyrs, above all, that this Psalm is realized in luminous fashion: *Multi martyres talia passi sunt, sed nihil sic elucet quomodo caput martyrum.*[25]

In the hierarchy of the elect the cohort of martyrs is followed by the illustrious choir of pontiffs, *Almus sacerdotum chorus.*[26]

In these the unique priesthood of our Saviour shines forth and radiates with its most brilliant light, since in reality there is but one priesthood, that of the eternal Pontiff, that is, of the Son of God become flesh. These great popes, these illustrious bishops whose memory the Church honors successively in the course of the liturgical year, have never accomplished anything except "through the virtue of the Spirit of Christ with which they are filled and which envelops them on all sides." [27] It is, moreover, the Holy Ghost Himself who charged them to rule and to tend to the Church that God has purchased through His blood.[28]

So let us not be surprised that the Church, from one end to the other of the office of the bishop confessors, glorifies the sovereign Priest, the *Sacerdos magnus,* who will never have found His like on earth. Who does not see that the Mass *Statuit,* for example, according to its different parts, relates to the priesthood of Jesus Christ? Upon what, then, does the Epistle *Ecce sacerdos magnus* shed light if it is not the pre-eminent greatness of the Pontiff whom the greatest personages of the Old Testament prefigured? [29]

It is still Jesus Christ whom we find and whom we glorify in these illustrious doctors of the Church whom the Spirit of God fills with wisdom and knowledge so that the divine light of Him who was given to us as the true Light of this world will always shine forth here below through them. Do we not on every feast of a doctor of the Church sing this beautiful antiphon of the Introit: *In medio Ecclesiae aperuit os ejus et implevit eum Dominus Spiritu sapientae et intellectus*? "And in the midst of the Church he shall open his mouth, and the Lord shall fill him with the spirit of wisdom and understanding." [30]

As for the simple confessors, whatever their condition on earth may have been, the Church does well to stress how, through the Spirit of Christ living in them, they resemble Jesus, the model Servant and the perfect Just Man of whom it was written: "The just shall flourish like the palm tree: he shall grow up like the cedar of Libanus." *Justus ut palma florebit; sicut cedrus Libani multiplicabitur.*[31]

With the virgins we breathe the very pure fragrance of Him who was the Son of Virginity. But, moreover, each virgin — and this is above all true for the Virgin of virgins — personifies the living Church, who since Pentecost is awaiting her Bridegroom; and each virgin represents the Church's characteristic traits: prudence and simplicity, sweetness and firmness. Thus it does not seem too much to assert that, in the liturgy of the virgins, martyrs and non-martyrs, it is the Church who is portraying herself according as the Holy Ghost guides her here below and prepares her for the day of the eternal nuptials with the Lamb of God.

As for the common of the women saints, it gives prominence to the wholly maternal activity of the Church and her vigilant solicitude. In this regard nothing is more significant than the epistle *Mulierem fortem*, which so well sets in relief the grateful appreciation owed to her by all her children: *Surrexerunt filii ejus et beatissimam praedicaverunt.*[32]

"Virgins," wrote Bossuet, "honor the Church through their state of purity, and married women through their fecundity; widows honor her through their widowhood, which is the state in which Jesus Christ left her upon withdrawing from the world."

Thus all the honors that we pay to the Saints rise as far up as Christ, who sits invisibly at the height of heaven but who, since Pentecost and by virtue of His Spirit, manifests Himself and clothes Himself in each one of His elect: *Mirabilis Deus in sanctis suis.*[33] This is precisely what is set off in the fullest light by the last great feast of the Christian year, All Saints' Day, whose liturgy, which admirably gives prominence to the most beautiful texts of the Apocalypse, unfolds around the Lamb immolated yet victorious — the paschal Lamb. Although figuring, quite naturally, among the feast of the Saints, the feast of All Saints very certainly is linked to the great solemnities of the redemptive mystery, since its veritable subject is the triumph of Christ in the plenitude of His Mystical Body. If, therefore, on the day of Pentecost, we celebrate the Holy Ghost giving birth to the Church, on All Saints' Day we further celebrate this same vivifying Spirit from whom the Church continues to receive her admirable fecundity.

In the preceding pages we have seen that, in each of the Saints whose memory it has us honor, the Church celebrates Christ, who, since Pentecost and by virtue of His Spirit, the sanctifying Spirit, continuously manifests His power and glory to the world. When we take this point of view, we understand without any difficulty how advantageous it is, in order to honor the Saints, to unite ourselves with the devotion which the Church itself offers them in her liturgy. Now, when it honors the Saints, the Church never neglects to offer thanks to Him who is the veritable author of the victory achieved by her elect. What was done in the first centuries to celebrate the memory of this or that martyr? On the anniversary day of the Saint's death, or, to speak more precisely, on the day of the Saint's birthday, in heaven, Christians assembled at the place where the martyrs' relics were preserved, and, after a vigil of prayers, they participated in the sacrifice of the Mass offered on the grave of the Saint in order to offer thanks to God for the Saint's triumph. Therefore today we could do nothing better to celebrate the feast of a Saint than to unite ourselves to the Sacrifice offered in his or her honor, but in order to render homage to God Himself, who, in the triumph of His elect, always manifests the victory of His grace. It is to Christ, to the merits of the Cross, to the pouring out of His Spirit that the Saints owe all that earned them entry to glory: their privileged vocation, the heroicity of their virtues, their fidelity to grace, and their own triumph here below. A versicle which often recurs in the office of the confessors marvelously summarizes the work accomplished by the Lord Himself in each one of His saints: *Amavit eum Dominus, et ornavit eum; stolam gloriae, induit eum.* In fact, it is certainly the Lord who loved with a love of predilection the Saint who is being memorialized. It is He who adorned him with His grace and His gifts; it is He who has clothed him in the glory which the Saint now enjoys in heaven.

This is why such a great number of liturgical texts for Saints' feasts direct our thanksgiving and praise to the Lord Himself. It is always God whom the Church glorifies in her elect. She makes this very clear in the Prefaces which were composed in honor of this or that Saint: "It is truly right and just, proper and helpful toward salvation that we always and everywhere give thanks to you, O Lord, holy Father, almighty and eternal God; and praise, honor, and extol You on this feast of the Blessed Mary ever Virgin." An ancient Preface in honor of Pope St. Sixtus, whose devotion was once so dear to the Roman Church, reads as follows: "It is truly right and just to give Thee thanks everywhere and always, but above all on the solemnity of this day in which the blessed Sixtus, pontiff and martyr, joyously offered Thee the effusion of his blood."

How many antiphons and responses, either in the Mass or in the office, glorify the Lord for the marvels that He has wrought in His saints. In the introit *Gaudens gaudebo*, of December 8, it is the Immaculate Virgin who herself recognizes that she has received from God this beauty without blemish whose praises we sing. "I shall rejoice in the Lord, and my soul shall exult in my God: for He has clothed me in the garments of salvation, and He has enveloped me in the mantle of justice, like a bride adorned with her jewels."

In a number of antiphons and responses, it is the Saints themselves who thank the Lord for the triumph they have achieved on earth. (Introit *Sacerdotes Dei* of the Mass of a Martyr Pontiff; Introit *Sancti tui* of the Mass of Several Martyrs in the paschal time, etc.).

It is all the more equitable on our part to thank the Lord for the spiritual riches with which He has filled His elect, that He gives them to us not only as models capable of sweeping us up by the example of their courage and virtue, but still more as powerful intercessors and vigilant protectors. It is likewise fitting that we know how to express our gratitude towards God for the joy that the feasts of Saints bring us, and the graces flowing therefrom, as the Church frequently suggests to us herself.

While offering thanks to God for the marvels that He Himself realized in each of His elect, the Church is careful — this goes without saying — not to neglect the personal merits and the virtues of the Saints. In her liturgical texts she does not fail to give prominence to the courage of martyrs, the fidelity and prudence of confessors, the wisdom and purity of virgins. But here, still, it is the holiness itself of Christ which the Church sees reflected in the virtues that we glorify in the Saints. Undoubtedly Christ is our perfect Model; however, He Himself manifested

Himself only on a very small point of the globe, and He lived, humble and hidden, among us only for a very few years. It will soon be twenty centuries since the Saviour removed Himself from our sight. But we find Him again in each one of those innumerable Saints who have followed one another in the course of the ages only to manifest the holiness of the sovereign Model under its different aspects. By continuing Himself this way in His Saints, the Saviour makes Himself accessible to all men of all times. If the conditions of existence today are very different from those that prevailed in the first century of our era, the example of the Saints proves to us that it is always possible to reproduce Christ by living according to His Spirit, no matter what the changes in customs or the difference of circumstances.

Do we wish to find the Saviour again in his dolorous Passion? Let us look at the martyrs. Do we wish to see Him again in His retreat in the desert? Let us seek Him in that multitude of anchorite Saints and monks who abandoned the world to take refuge in solitude and occupy themselves with prayer. Do we wish to join the divine Master preaching the coming of the kingdom of God on the roads of Galilee? We recognize Him easily in the heroism of those great missionaries of the Faith who, in similar conditions, evangelized the different peoples of the earth.

If the Church makes us recognize and honor this or that aspect of the holiness of the Saviour, in each of the elect that she proposes for our devotion, she also invites us to invoke them with all the more trust since they hold their power from Christ Himself. Nobody is unaware of the value that the Church attaches to the intercession of the Saints, nor the place that she reserves to it in her liturgical prayer. She does not proceed to any function of some importance without first petitioning the suffrage of the Saints. To base oneself humbly on the intercession of the Saints is to recognize the power that these privileged members of Christ enjoy in heaven, but which they dispose of, themselves, only to set the unfathomable riches of divine mercy in even greater relief.

Nothing is more legitimate than the invoking of Saints in order to obtain certain temporal benefits through their intercession, above all when some advantages of a spiritual order may derive from such benefits. Nonetheless, the role of Saints being to co-operate in the glorification of God for the definitive coming of His kingdom, it is fitting to follow the example of the Church herself by petitioning them preferably for graces which have some relation to their mission here below, or with the character peculiar to their holiness. It is an entirely normal thing to address oneself to St. John the Baptist, Precursor of the Messias and witness to the Lamb, to obtain a deeper and more intimate knowledge of the mysteries of Christ; to ask the martyr Saints for the grace to imitate their courage and their patience; and to ask the virgins for the grace of imitating their purity of soul and body.

Our piety towards the Saints will always be all the more strong and fruitful the more we model it on that of the Church. Now the more the elect reflect the holiness of the Redeemer, the higher are the liturgical honors that the Church bestows upon them. This is the idea behind the privileged devotion that we render to the Mother of Christ, the Virgin Mary, who surpasses all the angels of heaven and all the Saints of the earth in dignity. Undoubtedly it is very legitimate to have a certain preference for Saints, male and female, who have lived close to us and whose example touches us most directly. The mission with which St. Therese of Lisieux, a veritable model of evangelical simplicity, was providentially charged — precisely in the interest of a century such as ours is — suffices to justify the extraordinary and rapid diffusion of her devotion. It is very proper that each Christian attach himself more particularly to the Saint of his Baptism, the one from whom he must claim protection. It is entirely natural to address oneself more willingly to the patron of one's parish, or one's country, or one's trade. Religious cannot be reproached for greater devotion to the Saint who founded the order or institute to which they belong in and whom they rightly consider as their "Father." These different preferences, provided for by the Church, are perfectly justified and very much in conformity with the liturgical spirit.

Nonetheless it is important that these preferences, legitimate as they may be, be of no detriment to the devotion which, since antiquity, the Church has never ceased to render to those Saints who were the most closely united with the person of Christ in the work of our Redemption. Is this not notably the case with St. John the Baptist, and the Apostles? In regard to St. John the Baptist one can only deplore the distressing decadence of devoton to him, which formerly was justly popular. The disaffection of the Christian people in regard to the Precursor of Christ evidently derives from a complete misunderstanding of his role in the economy of our salvation and from a forgetfulness of his bond with the Saviour, a bond that is so close, according to Bourdaloue, that one cannot know Jesus well without knowing John. Would it not be very desirable that the piety of the faithful should likewise give a greater place to the holy Apostles and to great martyrs like St. Stephen and St. Lawrence? Why neglect the devotion of those who are sometimes called "the old Saints," as if they were no longer of our time? No, Saints do not grow old. The Saints of yesterday are still those of today. Let us honor and invoke them with all the trust that the Church herself evinces for them.

NOTES TO CHAPTERS

Part One

I

1. Cf. *Le Triomphe de Pâques*, Chap. I, La Cinquantaine pascale, p. 16.
2. Col., 3:1.
3. Secret prayer of the third Sunday after Easter.
4. *Omnipotens sempiterne Deus, qui paschalis solemnitatis arcanum hodierni mysterii plenitudine perfecisti.* Collect of the Leonine Sacramentary for the Feast of Pentecost (P.L., 55, 41).

2

1. It was fitting that, for Holy Week and the paschal Octave, the Church took from the four Gospels in succession everything that concerned the Passion and the Resurrection.
2. On Whitsunday we have the account of the appearance of Christ to St. Thomas (John 20:19–31), an appearance which took place on the eighth day after the Resurrection; on the following Sunday we have the Gospel of the Good Shepherd, which is completely natural.
3. The Gospel of the fourth Sunday (John 16:5–14) should regularly precede the one of the third Sunday (John 16:16–22). This transposition, which is found in the most ancient documents, seems quite intentional. Undoubtedly it must have seemed more logical to let the announcement of the Lord's departure for His Father's abode be read before reading the promise relating to the sending of the Paraclete.
4. The Church, therefore, rightly has the prayer called Christ's priestly

prayer read on the Eve of the Ascension. According to St. John this prayer immediately preceded Christ's passion (John 17:1–11).

5. The antiphon of the Communion of the Third Sunday, the antiphons of the *Magnificat* (First Vespers) and of the *Benedictus* of the same Sunday; the antiphons of the *Benedictus* and *Magnificat* (Second Vespers) of the Fourth Sunday; the antiphon of the *Magnificat* of Monday following the Fourth Sunday; the alleluiatic versicle of the Fifth Sunday; the antiphon of the *Magnificat* of Tuesday after the Fifth Sunday.

6. *In Joan.*, tr. 101, n. 6. St. Augustine's interpretation is not favored by most modern exegetes. According to them, the Saviour wished to say to His disciples: "You will be deprived of my presence during my Passion and my stay in the tomb, but immediately after my Resurrection you will see me again." This is not the place to discuss why we prefer St. Augustine's interpretation, an interpretation which has been held by such a knowledgeable commentator as Maldonatus. The latter asserts the validity of many arguments that have lost none of their pertinence and which merit being taken into consideration. We content ourselves with noting that St. Augustine's interpretation is proposed to us here by the Church Herself and that it accords perfectly with the paschal liturgy, which never loses sight of the Saviour's return at the end of days.

7. *Hoc modicum longum nobis videtur, quoniam adhoc agitur; cum finitum fuerit tunc sentiemus, quam modicum fuerit.*

8. The liturgical reading has retained only the first part of the last verse, which ends thus, "And in that day you shall ask me nothing." This can be understood only as the day of eternity, as St. Augustine thinks, and not as the time following the Resurrection.

3

1. At the end of Chapter 15 and the beginning of Chapter 16 of the Gospel of St. John, Christ tells His Apostles of the persecutions which await them at the hands of the Jews. It can be noted that the Gospel of this Fourth Sunday (John, 16:5–14 very logically follows the Gospel (John, 16:16-20) of the preceding Sunday despite the inversion mentioned above. After having announced that the disciples would soon no longer see Him, the Lord gives them the reason for His departure.

2. Generally the Greek term ὁ παράκλητος is translated as "The Consoler," "The Advocate," or again as "The Defender." But in truth

none of the words exactly express the sense of the Greek term as
employed here by St. John. In the thought of the Evangelist
παράκλητος designates the Holy Ghost as the one who internally
assists the members of the Church and who works in each one of
them.

3. "But you disowned the Holy and Just One," says St. Peter to the
   Jews (Acts, 3:14).

4. "From Him you are in Christ Jesus, Who has become for us God-
   given wisdom, and justice, and sanctification and Redemption,"
   writes St. Paul (1 Cor., 1:30).

5. The Paraclete, says Christ, "will convict the world of justice, because
   I go to the Father, and you will see me no more." The last words
   "and you will see me no more" complete the affirmation, "because I
   go to My Father." In fact the work of our justification, to which the
   Holy Ghost will bear witness, will manifestly be accomplished
   through Christ, when He will no longer be seen here below, having
   ascended to His Father.

6. John, 12:31–32. There is no need to recall that in this passage of the
   Gospel the Saviour is not so much alluding to His crucifixion as to
   His glorification, of which the Passion will have been only the first
   stage.

7. This is seen clearly by the question that the Apostles will put to
   Christ even at the moment of His Ascension. Cf. Acts, 1:6.

8. The Lord had specifically given His disciples to understand that the
   Holy Ghost would complete His teaching, and that the Holy Ghost
   would bring to their minds (ὑπομνήσει) whatever He had said to them.

9. The Greek text reads: "When this Spirit of truth will come, He will
   introduce you to the whole truth like a guide (ὁδηγήσει . . . εἰς)."

10. Christian theology rightly bases itself on this verse in order to estab-
    lish that the Holy Ghost proceeds from the Father and from the Son,
    and not only from the Father, although here it is directly only a
    question of the temporal mission of the Paraclete, and not of His
    eternal relation with the Son.

11. John, 14:9.

12. When Christ said to His disciples: "The hour is coming when I will
    no longer speak to you in parables, but will speak to you plainly of
    the Father," He is not alluding to the talks that will follow the
    Resurrection, and which St. John does not even mention. Here it
    can be a question only of this interior teaching that the Master will
    give His Apostles when, having made Himself spiritually present in
    each one of them on the day of Pentecost, He will communicate His
    own knowledge of the Father to them — that is to say, a filial knowl-

edge. It is in fact from the beginning of Pentecost, and thanks to the Holy Ghost living in them, that the disciples will know that Christ is in His Father, they in Him, and He in them. *In illo Die, vos cognoscetis quia ego sum in Patre Meo, et vos in Me, et ego in vobis* (John, 14:20).

13. Here Christ does not mean that He will cease to intercede on our behalf after His Ascension. In this matter the doctrine of St. John is no less clear than that of St. Paul (Cf. I John, 2:1); but the intercession of Christ glorified will be entirely different from what it was on earth. He will no longer petition in our place, but our prayer will rest on his merits and on His sovereign authority. In her liturgical prayer the Church never addresses herself to the Father without offering as a recommendation of herself the Son "Who lives and reigns with Him in the unity of the Holy Ghost."

4

1. Acts, 1:3.
2. Jean Daniélou, *Le symbolisme des quarante jours,* in *La Maison-Dieu,* 31, 1952, p. 19.
3. Gen., 7:4, 12, 17.
4. Numbers, 32:13; Deut., 2:7; 8:2–4; Exod., 16:35.
5. 1 Kings, 17:16.
6. Exod., 34:27, 28; Deut., 9:11.
7. The Lenten Epistles were regularly taken, save on Sunday, from the Old Testament. Those of the paschal time are all taken from the New. At Whitsuntide first the Acts of the Apostles are read, then the Catholic epistles. We begin with the reading of St. Peter (Easter Friday and Saturday). Then we read St. John (Whitsunday). We return to St. Peter (the second and third Sunday after Easter). Then we go on to St. James (fourth and fifth Sunday). Finally, the Sunday Epistle in the octave of the Ascension is again taken from St. Peter. There is a desirable and very apparent harmony between the passages which serve for readings during Mass and the liturgy of the last Sundays after Easter. The transpositions that we find there are not accidental.
8. This, of course, does not mean that Christians must submit to laws that are manifestly unjust, or contrary to the rights of God and His Church.
9. Secret of the fifth Sunday after Easter.

5

1. Secret of the Mass of the Ascension.
2. More than one liturgical text describes the Passion as "glorious." In the feast of the exaltation of the Holy Cross, we read, in one of the responses of Matins: *Tuam gloriosam recolimus passionem.* In the preface of the Roman Pontifical for the blessing of a new cross, the Passion is called "the very victorious Passion," *victoriossima passio.*
3. Hymn *Vexilla Regis*, 3rd verse.
4. Luke, 24:50–51.
5. Acts, 1:9.
6. Acts, 1:11.
7. Communicantes of the Mass.
8. John, 17:5. The entire passage is used as the Gospel of the Mass of the Vigil of the Ascension.
9. Phil., 2:9.
10. John, 14:28.
11. See Dom Vonier's *The Victory of Christ*, where a revealing light is shed on the teaching of Scripture and of Tradition on this subject.
12. See John, 17:1. Cf. the Epistle of the Vigil of the Ascension.
13. Eph., 1:10.
14. Eph., 1:19–21.
15. Eph., 2:5–7; St. Paul presents our glorification in Christ as something assured and already realized in principle. Hence the use of the perfect tense: *Et conresuscitavit, et consedere fecit in coelestibus.*
16. Phil., 2:11, which in the Greek text is "Jesus Christ is Lord *for* the glory (εἰς δόξαν) of God the Father."
17. Sermo 1, *De Ascensione Domini*, n. 4. This entire passage, as is fitting, is read at Matins of the Ascension (6th lesson).
18. John, 12:32. It cannot be repeated too often that these words of the Saviour relate more directly to the Ascension than to the crucifixion itself. The Jews seemed to have clearly understood it in this way, since they replied, "We have heard from the Law that the Christ abides forever." As regards St. John's remark, "Now He said this signifying by what death He was to die," it does not refer to the kind of final agony, but to the glorious character of the death itself, which is only the beginning of His exaltation.
19. Gay, *De la vie et des virtus crétiennes*, 1, Chap. V: De l'espérance chrétienne.

6

1. *Dictionnaire de la langue française.*
2. First antiphon of Vespers of the Octave of Christmas.
3. The significant change in the liturgical text will be noted here. *"Quid admiramini aspicientes"* instead of the *"Quid statis aspicientes"* of the scriptural text. Moreover, the accent of the melody is deliberately placed on *admiramini.*
4. Matins, the first antiphon of the first nocturn.
5. Matins, eighth response.
6. Matins, first antiphon of the second nocturn.
7. Matins, second antiphon of the first nocturn.
8. Matins, first antiphon of the third nocturn.
9. Matins, second antiphon of the third nocturn.
10. Matins, third antiphon of the third nocturn.
11. The 46th Psalm is the Psalm of the Introit of the Mass of the Ascension. It is used until Pentecost as the Psalm of thanksgiving after the main meal. The sixth verse, which appears in the Mass of the Ascension as an alleluiatic verse and as an antiphon of the Offertory, is used many times in the Office under different forms.

7

1. This expression appears in an article, an excellent one in other respects, on *The Mystery of Pentecost,* published several years ago.
2. Luke, 24:52.
3. Serm. 1, *De Ascensione Domini,* 4 (P.L., 54, 396).
4. John, 14:18.
5. *Loc. cit.*

8

1. *Journal de voyage,* French tr., p. 249.
2. *De vita Constantini,* 4, 64; P.G., 20, 1220.
3. *De solemnitate paschali,* 5; P.G., 24, 700.
4. Serm. 60; P.L., 49, 1194.
5. The first evidence of a feast of the Ascension celebrated on the fortieth day are probably the sermons of Saint John Chrysostom in the East and of Saint Augustine in the West on the subject of this solemnity, though both Saints considered such a feast already ancient and universally accepted.

6. Can. 43. Cassian, too, in this twentieth conference, declares for keeping the connection between the Ascension and the ten days between
   it and Pentecost, so as to keep the same festive spirit alive during
   the whole fifty days.
7. John, 16:7.
8. Acts, 2:32, 33.
9. *The Victory of Christ (La victoire du Christ)*, French trans., p. 121.

Part Two

9

1. It is thus designated in the Gregorian Sacramentary.
2. *Ordo romanus* XI, P.L., 78, 1049. According to this some *Ordo*, which
   dates from the Middle Ages, the Sunday after Ascension was called
   "Sunday of the Rose," because a shower of roses was poured down
   from the vaults of the church (symbolizing the pouring out of the
   Holy Ghost) during the Mass, and while the Pope was preaching on
   the coming of the Paraclete.
3. Ps. 26:7, 8, 9.
4. "God shall reign over the nations: God sitteth on His holy throne."
   This versicle, like the antiphon of the Offertory, is taken from the
   46th Psalm, the Psalm of the Ascension.
5. "God is ascended with jubilee, and the Lord with the sound of
   trumpets."
6. It is useful to remark that the passage from the Gospel that is read
   on the Sunday after the Ascension immediately precedes the entire
   chapter that is read in the course of the three Sundays after Easter.
   Whereas the Gospel of the Sunday after the Ascension is composed
   of the first verses of Chapter 16 (John, 15:26; 16:1–4), the Gospels
   of the three preceding Sundays give the rest of the same chapter. It
   seems very unlikely that a transposition of this kind is accidental.
7. John 15:26.
8. John, 16:2–4.
9. John, 17:12, 13, 15.
10. "Cleanse us through this spotless offering, O Lord, and let our souls
    be made strong by your heavenly grace."
11. 1 Peter, 4:8.
12. 1 Peter 4:9–11.
13. Acts, 4:32.

14. John, 13:35.
15. "O Almighty and eternal God, make our wills devoted to you so that our hearts may sincerely serve your majesty."
16. *Christ, the Ideal of the Monk* (*Le Christ, ideal du moine*), French trans., p. 445.
17. 1 Cor. 6:19.
18. *Memento, Domine, . . . Omnium circumstantium quorum tibi fides cognita est et nota devotio.* Memento of the Living.
19. Collect of the fifth Sunday after Easter.
20. Epistle of the Sunday.

10

1. Canon of the Mass, Communicantes of the Ascension.
2. Ezech., 36:26–27.
3. Joel, 2:28. Cf. Matins of Pentecost, lessons of the first nocturn; Ember Wednesday, First Lesson of the Mass.
4. Mark, 1:8.
5. Acts, 1, 5.
6. John 16:7. Before this (John 14:16) Christ had contented Himself with telling His Apostles that, at His request, the Father would send another Paraclete: *Ego rogabo Patrem, et alium Paraclitum dabit vobis.* In this passage He tells them that He Himself will send the Paraclete: *mittam eum ad vos.*
7. Acts, 2:33.
8. *The Victory of Christ*, French trans., p. 114.
9. Dom Vonier, *The New and Eternal Covenant* (*La nouvelle et eternelle Alliance*), French trans., p. 69.
10. John, 14:18.
11. Math. 28:20.
12. There is no lack today of pious souls who are troubled because they do not sufficiently know the Holy Ghost, and who complain that theologians and preachers do not speak sufficiently about Him. It seems to them that of the Three Divine Persons, the Holy Ghost is the most often sacrificed. One could reply to such souls with the very beautiful pages written by Théodore de Régnon under the title, *De la devotion au Saint-Esprit.* "Reassure yourselves, then, souls so devoted to Jesus, and do not believe yourselves obliged to share your adorations. For to praise Jesus is to praise His perfection and the perfection of Jesus is the Holy Ghost. Persevere then in concentrating on Jesus, nothing but Jesus, plunge forward as far as possible into the

interior of Jesus. It is there that you will attain, that you will know, that you will adore the Spirit who proceeds from the Father and who is the Spirit of the Son, as Saint John Damascene says — the Spirit who proceeds from the Son and who dwells in Him, as Saint Cyril says." (*Etudes de théologie positive*, t. 3., p. 171). Nothing is more conformable with the doctrine of the Church Fathers, and with the liturgy itself, which, in all its feasts, from Christmas to Pentecost, celebrates exclusively the mystery of Christ. If the Son became incarnated, it was precisely for the reason, as is sung in the preface to Christmas, of sweeping us up into the love of the invisible things: *Ut dum visibiliter Deum cognoscimus, per nunc in invisibilium amorem rapiamur.*

II

1. Introit of the Sunday of the Octave of Christmas.
2. Acts, 2:1–14; the account in the Acts of the Apostles is read on the day of Pentecost, in the night office and in the Mass of the Feast.
3. The group of persons gathered around St. Peter at the moment of the election of St. Matthias numbered "about a hundred and twenty." It was probably the same group that was at the Cenacle on the day of Pentecost.
4. The crowd was undoubtedly attracted by the confused noise which rose from the Cenacle (*facta autem hac voce, convenit multitudo*). In fact immediately after the pouring out of the Holy Ghost, and under His inspiration, the disciples began to proclaim the *Magnalia Dei*. It seems improbable that in this circumstance the disciples had made use of multiple foreign languages, which would have produced a singular cacaphony. In all probability they were expressing themselves in an ecstatic way, and in a mysterious language, in which, through a particular grace, the bearers were able to perceive the meaning, As André Rétif has written recently: "Substantially the phenomenon would not be different from the charism known by the name of glossalaly." Cf. *La Mystère de la Pentecôte*, in *La Vie Spirituelle*, 1951, p. 462.
5. Thus the hymns of Matins and Lauds; the greater part of the night office; many versicles and antiphons of the office of the day, notably the antiphon *Hodie* of the Magnificat (second Vespers); the Communion of the Mass: *Factus est repente*, etc.
6. . . . *et diem sacratissimum celebrantes quo Spiritus Sanctus apostolis innumeris linguis apparuit.*
7. Wisdom, 1:7.

12

1. Acts 2:1. We say, "perhaps," because the expression employed by St. Luke, and which the Vulgate translates *Cum complerentur dies Pentecostes*, could also mean, "And whereas the day of Pentecost had arrived." Cf. Pirot and Clamer, *La Sainte Bible*, i. XI, p. 50.
2. De baptismo, C. 19; *De corona militis*, C. 3; *De oratione*, C. 23.
3. Origen already gives the fiftieth day the name of *Pentecostes*. Cf. *Adv. Celsum* 8, 9.
4. Can. 43. Cf. Héfélé, *Histoire des Conciles*, 1, 1, p. 245.
5. *Hodie tandem ad ipsum culmen honorum provecti Sumus, ad ipsam metropolitim festorum evasimus, ad fructum ipsum dominicae promissionis parvenimus. Homilia secunda de sancta Pentecostes*, P.G., 50, 463.
6. P.L., 55, 39.

13

1. Acts, 1:6.
2. Mark, 16:14.
3. John, 14:26. The Holy Ghost will recall the teaching of Christ, but by presenting it in a new light.
4. John, 16:13.
5. "So they departed from the presence of the Sanhedrin, rejoicing that they had been counted worthy to suffer disgrace for the name of Jesus." (Acts 5:41).
6. Acts, 4:32.
7. The Church Fathers frequently compared Pentecost with Babel. Numerous allusions to the comparison could also be found in the ancient liturgies.

14

1. 1 Cor., 6:19.
2. We leave to theologians a discussion of the exact nature of the presence — certainly a substantial and very intimate one — which Scripture attributes to the Person of the Holy Ghost. Let us say here that it is essentially different from the presence "of immensity," according to which, by His action, God is present to all His visible and invisible creatures, in heaven, on earth, and even in hell. "The manner in which God became man," sagely writes Dom Vonier, "is a secret that

God has not revealed; the mode of habitation of the Holy Ghost in the souls of the just is another secret kept by God; but in the two cases, both sublime, it is literally true that one Divine Person, and not another Person, has descended from heaven to dwell with man on earth." *The New and Eternal Covenant*, French trans., p. 66.

3. It is not enough to call the Holy Ghost "the guest of the soul." This appellation appears, it is true, in the Sequence of Pentecost, but it is habitually employed neither among the Fathers, nor in the liturgy.

4. St. Athanasius, *First Letter to Serapion*, n. 20 (cf. Théodore de Régnon, *Etudes de théologie positive sur la Sainte Trinité*, t. IV, pp. 437 and 55).

5. Second alleluiatic versicle of the Mass.

6. Sequence of the Mass.

7. This Collect relates more directly to the neophytes who are "reborn" in the night of Pentecost. In it there is a reference to Confirmation which follows Baptism. The "splendor claritatis" recalls the *splendor gloriae* of the Epistle to the Hebrews, 2:3, and the "lux tuae lucis," the *Lumen de Lumine* of our Nicene Creed. The light which emanates from the Father, and which the Son transmits, penetrates us only through the illumination of the Holy Ghost.

8. *Praesta, quaesumus, omnipotens Deus, ut Spiritus adveniens, majestatem nobis Filii tui manifestando clarificet.*

9. In antiquity it was forbidden to pray on one's knees during the fifty-day paschal period. This prohibition was still severely maintained by the first Council of Nicea (can. 20).

10. This is the second alleluiatic versicle. This piece is of a venerable antiquity, since it is already found in very ancient manuscripts. "It is an original composition of great beauty," says Dom Gajard. "Widely known, it endured, words and melody, down the ages as the very model of invocation to the Holy Ghost, because of the fervor of intense supplication with which it is filled." *La messe de Pentecôte* in the *Revue grégorienne*, May–June, 1953, p. 100.

11. *Illo nos igne, quaesumus Domine, Spiritus Sanctus inflammet quem Dominus noster Jesus Christus misit in terram et voluit vehementer accendi.* Second Collect of Ember Saturday.

12. The *Veni Creator* is sung during the Octave of Pentecost, not only at Vespers but also at Tierce.

13. Secret prayer and Postcommunion of Pentecost, the Collect of Tuesday after Pentecost, etc.

14. "Almighty and merciful God, grant that the Holy Spirit may come and dwell in us, that we may be a temple of his glory."

15. Postcommunion prayer of the two Easter Masses.

15

1. Cf. *Le triomphe de Pâques*, 69 ff.
2. Acts, 2:41. St. Leo justly points out the example of St. Peter on behalf of Pentecost (Ep. 16: P. L., 54, 699).
3. P. L., 13, 1134.
4. Ep. 16; P. L., 54, 699. In another letter St. Leo likewise reproached the bishops of Campania and Picenum for administering Baptism, without necessity, outside the feasts of Easter and Pentecost.
5. Since the 15th century, different Western councils were opposed to children being confirmed before the age of seven. Benedict XIV in the *Constitution Eo quamvis tempore*, of May 4, 1745, established the claims of the practice of the Western Church.
6. *Codex juris canonici*, Can. 770.
7. Can. 788.
8. Can. 790.
9. Acts, 4:20.
10. Chap. 17, *Du sacrament de confirmation*, § 5, Des effets du sacrement.
11. Cf. A. M. Roguet: *Les sacrements, signes de vie*.
12. Eph., 5:8–9.
13. Phil., 2:15.
14. Acts, 2:4.
15. Eph. 5:18–20.
16. Roguet, *op. cit.*, p. 84.

16

1. *Laeti bibamus sobriam ebrietatem Spiritus*. (Hymn of Lauds on Monday.)
2. Acts, 2:46.
3. *The Victory of Christ*, French trans., p. 121.
4. Acts, 5:41.
5. Phil., 2:7.
6. In the office of the feast this Psalm is the second of three Matins Psalms. In the Mass it is the Introit, although today only the first verse of it is sung. Verses 29 and 30 form the antiphon of the Offertory. Psalm 67 is likewise suited to the feast of Ascension, which is not surprising, given the close link that exists between the two solemnities.
7. "Grant that through the same Holy Ghost we may be always truly wise and rejoice in his consolation." (The Collect of Pentecost).

17

1. The Octave of Pentecost already existed in Rome at the end of the 6th century, as is seen by the *Comes* of Wurzburg, which assigns readings proper to the different days of the week. Strictly speaking it is not an octave, since this complement of Pentecost actually lasts only seven days and not eight.

2. Several liturgists have expressed the wish to see the Octave of Pentecost disappear, notably Dom Odilon Heiming, O.S.B., in an article that was reproduced by *La Maison-Dieu,* under the title: *Réflexions sur la reforme du calendrier liturgique* (1952, pp. 106).

3. At the Mass of each day of the Octave, the Preface of Pentecost repeats, "On this day *(hodierna die)* he sent forth the Holy Spirit upon his adopted children, as he had promised." Likewise the Communicantes of the canon each day repeats the formula, *Diem sacratissimum celebrantes,* "celebrating the most sacred day of Pentecost."

4. According to St. Leo (Serm. 78), the Ember Days were carried out immediately after the expiration of the paschal time precisely in order to make reparation for the sins committed in the course of a period of the year in which penance was suspended. However, in the 6th century, when the week of Pentecost was made similar to the Octave of Easter, the fast of Ember Days was moved back one or several weeks. But such a fluctuation followed later, until the 11th century, in the fixing of the Summer Ember Days that Pope Gregory VII, in order to put an end to this state of affairs, decided that these Ember Days would always be celebrated during the Octave of Pentecost.

5. The same remark can be made with respect to the December Ember Days, the liturgy of which harmonizes perfectly with the ferias of Advent more especially consecrated to the joyous mysteries of the Annunciation and the Visitation.

6. Rupert: *De divinis officiis,* 10, 26; P.L., 170, 289. Durand de Mende gives a similar explanation in his *Rational.*

7. The Introit of the Friday of these same September Ember Days is likewise an invitation to joy: *Laetetur cor quarentium Dominum* ("Let the hearts of those who seek the Lord rejoice.") This is all the more significant since only the September Ember Days have preserved intact the liturgical tonality peculiar to the penitential ferias.

8. Serm. 2, *De jejunio decimi mensis,* P. L., 54, 172.

9. What would one think of an architect who, under the pretext of restoring a Roman edifice to its perfect purity of style, and by taking no account of the transformations that had taken place in following

centuries, would want radically to ban everything that the art of the Middle Ages and the Renaissance added to it? Let us distrust, above all when it is a question of worship, those reforms which proceed from conceptions that are too systematic and too rigid. Nothing needs to be treated with more discretion and tact than the liturgy.

10. The absence of a station at the basilica of St. Paul, the second patron of Rome, is easily explained. The Apostle of the Gentiles had not been at the Cenacle at the time of the descent of the Holy Ghost. He was converted and began his mission a long time after the first Pentecost.

11. This observation has already been made by Dom Morin in his article *Le lectionnaire de Wurzburg* (*Revue Bénédictine,* 1949, p. 46).

12. Joel, 2:28–32 (Cf. Acts, 2:4–21). All these readings of the Saturday of Pentecost derive from the Ember Days, as also does the Gospel. All the alleluiatic versicles come from the Octave and several Collects are taken from the Ember Days.

13. Lev., 23:9–17, 21.

14. Deut., 26:1–3, 7–11.

15. Lev., 26:3–12.

16. Joel, 2:23–24, 26–27.

17. Such, for example, as this versicle which follows the second lesson: *Spiritus ejus ornavit coelos.* "His Spirit has adorned the heavens." These few words taken from Job (26:13) become here an allusion to the charismatic gifts of the Holy Ghost poured over the Apostles (*coelos*).

18. The last words of this text of St. Paul (Rom., 5:5) have been slightly modified in the antiphon of the Introit. Instead of *Per Spiritum Sanctum qui datus est nobis,* the antiphon reads *Per inhabitantem Spiritum ejus in nobis.*

19. Second Collect of Ember Wednesday.

20. First Lesson of Ember Wednesday.

21. Epistles of Monday and Tuesday.

22. Epistle of Wednesday.

23. Gospels of Monday and Tuesday.

24. Gospel of Wednesday.

Part Three

18

1. Gal. 3:14. Cf. the article, "Croyons-nous au Saint-Esprit?" by S. B. in *La Vie Spirituelle*, May, 1953, p. 495.
2. This "truth" of which we often read in Scripture, and notably in St. John, is nothing else but the fidelity of God to His commitments towards Israel.
3. Although the Jews had never considered Pentecost as the anniversary of the promulgation of the Law on Mt. Sinai, the Church Fathers often compared the two events with each other: the gift of the Law on Mt. Sinai, and the pouring out of the Holy Ghost on the day of Pentecost, as did St. Leo in his first sermon on Pentecost, a passage from which figures in the Roman breviary in the Office of this feast.
4. *L'Esprit et L'Epouse*, French tr., p. 82. Perhaps it would be more exact to trace the birth of the Church to the time when the sacrifice of the Cross was realized. This was done by Leo XIII in his encyclical *Divinum Illud*, where he expressed himself as follows: "The Church, already conceived, and issued forth, so to speak, from the side of the new Adam asleep on the Cross, manifested herself for the first time in a brilliant manner on the solemn day of Pentecost." Pius XII in his encyclical on the Mystical Body repeated this sentence from Leo XIII. Dom Vonier has started out from another vantage point in that the Church, in his view, was born at the very moment when the pouring out of Pentecost rendered her fecund.
5. John, 14:16.
6. Collect *Pro omni gradu Ecclesiae*.
7. "For those who love you, O God, joys beyond understanding are waiting. Fill our hearts with such a love that our desire for you in all things, and above all things, may lead us to your promises, which are far superior to anything we can desire." (Collect of the Fifth Sunday after Pentecost.)
8. "Almighty and eternal God, deepen our Faith, our Hope and our Charity, so that we may attain what you have promised and love what you have commanded." (Collect of the Thirteenth Sunday after Pentecost.)
9. Collect of the Tenth Sunday.
10. Collect of the Twelfth Sunday.
11. Epistle of the Ninth Sunday (cf. 1 Cor., 10:16–13).
12. *Convivificavit nos in Christo . . . et conresuscitavit, et consedere fecit in coelestibus in Christo* (Eph., 2:6).

13. . . . *Deus, qui dedit nobis pignus Spiritus* (2 Cor., 5:5).

14. *Signati estis spiritu promissionis sancto qui est pignus hereditatis nostrae* (Eph., 1:13, 14).

15. Rom., 8:17.

16. The votive feast of Trinity Sunday being fixed for the first Sunday after Pentecost, the Mass of this Sunday can never be celebrated except during the week.

17. Ps. 16:6.

18. Collect of the Third Sunday.

19. Offertory of the Third Sunday.

20. Communion Hymn (antiphon) of the Eighth Sunday.

21. Gradual of the Fourteenth Sunday.

22. Alleluiatic versicle of the Sixth Sunday.

23. Gradual of the Eighth Sunday, Introit of the Fifteenth Sunday, Gradual of the Twentieth Sunday, etc.

24. Rom., 8:11.

25. Collect of the Sixteenth Sunday.

26. Collect of the First Sunday.

27. Collect of the Eighteenth Sunday.

28. Collect of the Third Sunday. Cf. likewise the Collects of the Eighth Sunday, of the Fourteenth, the Fifteenth, etc.

29. John, 15:5.

30. Cf. John, 16:13.

31. Hymn *Veni Creator Spiritus*; Cardinal Newman's translation.

19

1. John, 16:13.

2. Dom Vonier, *The Victory of Christ*, p. 119.

3. Ephes., 1:4.

4. Gal., 2:20.

5. Vespers, Feast of All Saints, third antiphon.

6. Common of a Confessor, first antiphon of Vespers.

7. "For star differs from star in glory" (1 Cor., 15:41).

8. John, 17:22.

9. During Advent the Gregorian Sacramentary admits only St. Lucy and St. Thomas the Apostle; during Lent it admits only St. Matthias, St. Gregory and the Annunciation of the Blessed Virgin.

10. It seems fully demonstrateed now that the organization of the Sundays after Pentecost is the work of St. Gregory. It was he, probably,

who divided the Sundays into three principal series: a first one after the feast of the Holy Apostles (*post natale apostolorum*), comprising six Sundays; a second after St. Lawrence (*post sancti Laurenti*) comprising seven Sundays; a third after St. Michael (*post sancti Angeli*) comprising eight Sundays. According to this arrangement the Sundays are stabilized between the three great feasts of the Roman Saints' days.

Fluctuation took place only during the period between Pentecost and June 29. One then used Masses which had not found a place in the paschal time. The feasts of Saints were not without influence on the Sunday liturgy. Undoubtedly it is not by chance that the Gospel account of the miraculous draught of fishes is read regularly as the feast of St. Peter approaches, and that the parable of the unjust steward recurs each year around the feast of St. Lawrence.

11. Gradual of the Mass *Intret*, for the Common of Many Martyrs.
12. The Feasts of the Apostles are all of the rite of the second class, and preceded by a Vigil.
13. *Isti sunt viri quos elegit Dominus in caritate non ficta* (Common of the Apostles, response of Matins).
14. *Jam non dicam vos servos . . . vos autem dixi amicos* (John, 15:15).
15. Common of the Apostles, response of Matins.
16. Common of the Apostles, response of Matins.
17. *Cohors triumphans martyrum* (Hymn of Lauds for All Saints' Day).
18. During the first three centuries, only the martyrs received honors of devotion. In the Canon of the Mass the Church mentions only martyrs, and in the Litany of the Saints she invokes them immediately after the Apostles. The liturgy of the martyrs, be it in the proper or in the common, is particularly rich and varied, above all during the fifty-day paschal period. Today, unfortunately, as a result of the multiplication of new feasts or of the importance given to more modern saints, many of the feasts of the martyrs are eclipsed, or reduced to a brief memorial, when they have not disappeared completely. What remains to us today of the feast of St. Sixtus, once so dear to Roman piety? Certain feasts that are most venerable and most interesting, like those of SS. Nereus and Achilleus, of SS. Gervase and Protase, etc., are regularly smothered. Would it not be possible to give greater prominence to the liturgy of martyrs, where the splendid texts remain as vital and timely as ever?
19. Acts, 6:10.
20. Mat., 10:20.
21. Acts, 7:55.
22. Common of Several Martyrs, response of Matins.

23. Common of Several Martyrs, Hymn of Lauds.
24. "Thou hast protected me, O Lord, from the assembly of the malignant; from the multitude of the workers of iniquity."
25. *In psalmum 63.*
26. Office of All Saints' Day, Hymn of Lauds.
27. Roman Pontifical, Preface to the consecration of a bishop.
28. *Spiritus sanctus posuit episcopos regere Ecclesiam Dei quam acquisivit sanguine suo* (Acts, 20:28).
29. This Epistle was taken from the Book of Ecclesiasticus (ch. 44 and 45), but the biblical text was greatly revised. Numerous verses have been omitted, abridged, or transposed. Many words have been changed or revised, and the sequence of the sentences has been modified. From this mosaic of texts that relate to Enoch, Noah, Abraham, Isaac, Jacob, Moses and Aaron in Scripture, the Church has been able to compose an admirable portrait of Christ, the unique Pontiff who in Himself possesses the fullness of sacerdotal holiness. Moreover, the *Statuit* Mass in reality celebrates the priesthood of Christ. The Introit, the Gradual, the alleluiatic versicle, the Offertory, and the Communion are properly and directly applicable to Christ, the eternal Pontiff.
30. Eccles., 15:5. It would be fitting to write "Spiritu" with a capital "S". In the liturgical text it is the Holy Ghost who is in question.
31. Ps. 91:13–14. Introit of the second Mass of a Confessor Not a Bishop.
32. "Her children rose up, and called her blessed" (Proverbs, 31:28).
33. Ps. 36:67. Offertory of the Mass *Intret*, of the Common of Several Martyrs.